THE POLITICS OF ARCHITECTURE

THE POLITICS OF ARCHITECTURE

A history of modern architecture in Britain

ANTHONY JACKSON

THE ARCHITECTURAL PRESS
LONDON

85139 529 5
First published 1970
© Architectural Press 1970

Printed in Great Britain by
Willmer Brothers Limited, Birkenhead

TO MY WIFE

While most of the research for this book was done in Britain and New York, I especially wish to thank Nova Scotia Technical College and its library for their help and encouragement.

CONTENTS

Illustrations will be found between pages 80 *and* 161, *and are listed on pages* 8-10.

The following abbreviations are used in the text:
RIBA Royal Institute of British Architects
AA Architectural Association

ILLUSTRATIONS

8

ACKNOWLEDGMENTS

Acknowledgments are due to those editors and publishers who have given permission for quotations to be made, and whose names appear in the References. Below are listed the sources of illustrations.

Ahrends, Burton & Koralek: 148b. Architectural Press: photo by Herbert Felton, 86. Photos by H. de Burgh Galwey, 133 b. 134 t, 134 b, 144 b, 150. Photo by Sam Lambert, 160 t. Photo by Millar & Harris, 132 t. Photo by Sydney W. Newbery, 89, 99. Photos by W. J. Toomey, 128, 137, 139 t, 139 b, 157. Photos by Dell & Wainwright, 93, 96 t, 96 b, 97, 101 t, 102, 103, 104. Photos not surviving, 82 b, 88, 90 b, 100 b, 107 b, 130. Brecht-Einzig Ltd: 147 t, 160 b. Casson, Conder & Partners: photo by Henk Snoek, 149. Chamberlin; Powell & Bon: photo by John Maltby, 143.
CLASP Development Group: photo by Keith Gibson, 154, photo by P. W. & L. Thompson, 152 t, 152 b. Leslie Collier: 133 t. Coventry Corporation: 155. John Donat: 147 c, 147 b, 148 t. C. C. Gillies: 98. G. L. C. 116 b, 120, 122, 136 b, 138 t, 140, 156. H. M. S. O: 123 b, 158 t, 142 b (MOHLG). Anthony Jackson: 83 t, 83 b, 90 t, 91 t, 92 t, 92 b, 100 t, 101 b, 107 t, 108, 111, 113, 121 t, 121 b, 123 t, 125 126 132 b. A. W. D. Lacey: photo by Colin Westwood, 151. Denys Lasdun & Partners, 144 t, 145 t, photo by Behr, photo by Brecht-Einzig Ltd, 159. Robert Matthew, Johnson-Marshall: 153. Museum of Modern Art, New York: 82 t. National Monuments Record: photos by Herbert Felton, 104 b, 106. Peter Pitt: 142 t. RIBA: 116 t. Alison & Peter Smithson: 136 top 2. Marilyn Stafford: 141. Stevenage Development Corporation: photo by G. L. Blake 155 t. L. Hugh Wilson: photo by Douglas Scott, 158 b.
t = top,   c = centre,   b = bottom.

1 PREVIEW

The Weissenhof exhibition of 1927, organized by the Deutscher Werkbund and directed by Ludwig Mies van der Rohe, was the culmination of the first phase of the development of modern architecture. Seventeen architects collaborated to produce a model garden suburb of sixty dwellings outside Stuttgart in Germany. No program of requirements or conditions of construction were laid down by the city authorities and Mies encouraged his colleagues to freely present their current researches. Mies himself designed a horizontal apartment block exploiting the flexibility of skeleton construction; J. J. P. Oud contributed a terrace of five small houses as a continuation of the work in low cost housing that he was engaged upon in Holland; Le Corbusier built a Citrohan house that was the latest of a series of projects that started in 1920; and Walter Gropius demonstrated his ideas on industrialization and prefabrication. The community was initially conceived by Mies as a related sequence of blocks on a terraced hill with pedestrian through ways opening into squares, but as the city wanted to sell the buildings separately at the end of the exhibition, they were built individually along conventional roadways. Nevertheless the general form of the community remained, unified by its consistency of design. Most of the group invited by Mies to collaborate on the exhibition were members of the *Ring*, an association of progressive Berlin architects formed in 1925, but six were from outside Germany including the Dutch Oud and Mart Stam, and the French Le Corbusier and his partner Pierre Jeanneret. These architects, together with Mies and Gropius, established the excellence of design that made Weissenhof internationally famous and, at the same time, by their participation, gave to the exhibition an international significance. For the first time the buildings of the European avant-garde were seen together and the result was conspicuously harmonious. Dutch, French, Belgian and Austrian used the same formal language as their German neighbours.

The architects who built at Weissenhof had developed from different influences and some of them were to quickly mature as distinctive personalities, but in 1927 they appeared to have produced a collective expression of the spirit of the time: the hollow perforated rectangular box became the popular symbol of modern architecture. This simplification grouped buildings that were subtly different. Le Corbusier's two buildings raised the volume off the ground on stilts and modelled the roof as a garden so that the form stood unfolded and complete. The buildings of Mies and Oud had no containment but their proportions. Oud's repetitive units were built up of cubic envelopes that had their thinness made apparent by visually located slots of glass. The apartment block of Mies used its glass as an infill between structural solids so that while it was more glazed than its neighbours, the resultant effect was of a monolithic slab. Only the lesser architects, and those of the older generation who had taken up the modern style, kept closely to the hole-in-the-wall aesthetic. For the Weissenhof exhibition was not just the manifesto of an avant-garde but almost a miniature history of the modern movement. Peter Behrens, fifty-eight years old, had done his pioneering work twenty years earlier; Gropius, Mies and Le Corbusier were all in their forties; Stam was only twenty-eight and of another generation.

At its most inventive, the new architecture was concerned with the exploitation of spatial sequences. Whether these be the horizontal flowing spaces of Mies, the three-dimensional modelling of Le Corbusier, or even the agglomeration of separate spaces by Gropius, the interiors had to be moved through to be experienced. The single volume was of less importance than the total effect of moving through the building. The independence of interior space and exterior form, where each takes on its own characteristics, gave way to a volumetric geometry with the outer skin as a simple expression of the inner configuration. The rationale of the form derived from the spaces; the success of the spaces was finally determined by the form. A regulating honesty prohibited deceptions at this juncture. No extraneous or concealed elements could alter an essentially mishandled plan formation or rather, no elements were permitted that could not be explained away. For the logic of the new architecture was more often symbolic than real.

Based upon a machine mythology, the aim was not just to imitate the technological process but to create a new species of modern objects. The modern architect extolled the virtues of the utilitarian engineer but copied him more in spirit than in practice. Appearances were more important than actuality. A material must seem suitable, a structure must seem logical, a form must seem reasonable. The resultant form might be close to the neo-Classical and the use of the structure little more advanced than the Greek, but architecture took on the clean-cut complexion of the machine and regardless of whether the concrete-looking skin covered brick, wood, steel—or concrete, the new architecture took its place with those turbines and grain elevators that were the unconscious symbols of the age. The machine portrayed the new life uncluttered by either the primitive past or the messiness of human sentimentality. Modern architecture stood by the automobile and the aeroplane and tried to look like an emanation from the Zeitgeist. This universality, the desire to bring into existence a building style of general application, as suitable for a dwelling as for a city, was completely against the residue philosophy of the nineteenth century that insisted upon differing styles for differing functions. Erich Mendelsohn's expressionist attempt to evoke machine shapes out of building content was condemned by the majority of his contemporaries who wanted a universal architecture that would ignore personality and speciality.

Manhattan was their Mecca though it contained no example of modern architecture. The Europeans were searching for an imagery; the Americans had found one without even looking. The skyscraper was a form born of its time, fashioned by the realities of the social economy, constructed in steel, serviced with elevators, occupied by the new class of white collar workers. When the design was unsullied by the idiosyncratic ornament of a Sullivan, the basic image stood inevitable in its cage-like simplicity. But this was still architecture at the level of engineering; the Europeans intended to raise it to the level of art.

Other than in its elemental statement of function, the skyscraper was of little visual interest, yet it contained in its building components elements akin to those of contemporary art. As with the de Stijl or Constructivist movements, its geometry was based upon the rectangle. Versatile in function, anonymous, flexible in scale, infinite in its possible combinations, the rectangular prism was the key to an international style. In the history of building, architecture had generally been limited by materials and techniques to the use of the primary geometric forms but for the twentieth century where everything was possible, a conscious renunciation made only the simplest acceptable. Yet this simplicity was illusory because the image was more painterly than architectural. In the skyscraper, the rectangular prism was made up of the orthodox building elements of floors, walls and roofs, brought together by the laws of structure. The modern architect desired the form but not the conventional concomitants of mass and gravity. Confronted by the formal interplay of abstract art, the architect expanded this vocabulary into the unreceptive elements of his own art form. Walls and floors and roofs had to become vertical and horizontal planes regardless of their constructional requirements. While it was simple enough to hide the structural horizontals, the verticals were more difficult to cope with. The use of a frame created its own problems where columns had to be integrated into the interior design or camouflaged, or often left unresolved. And while the outer wall became a simple skin, the necessities of weather control made its appearance unpleasantly substantial. Again the architect had to take corrective action, moving the window glass forward to conceal the depth of the wall. Finally, building materials themselves had to be released from their constructional overtones and so the ubiquitous stucco veneer covered the remains of ordinary building practice. Self-limited to his volumetric box, coloured as at Weissenhof with the white, green, grey, brown and blue of Le Corbusier or even the crimson, blue and yellow of Bruno Taut, the architect was able to explore form and space with almost the same freedom as the nonobjective artist.

The exterior form of the new architecture was a study in surface composition with movement suggested both on and perpendicular to the plane by the juxtaposition of opening and wall. While the void of the windows linked interior and exterior, as if the inside volume had been caged off from its spatial milieu, the transparency, sheen and reflectivity of the glass caused a more extended visual interpenetration. Against this perpendicular play of surfaces which held the building to its site, the lateral disposition of the pattern forced the viewer up and down and around the building. As the outside formal arrangement and inside spatial sequence gelled in the memory, the whole related to the logic of the program and was given an intellectual base. Form, space, structure, plan, came together into a unified architecture. Within this purity of expression, there was no place for further embellishment. The rejection of the traditional use of building materials and techniques eliminated the possibilities of conventional detail; the nature of the aesthetic prohibited applied decoration other than colour. In their place another range of motifs was developed which gave the necessary subsidiary interest. Stairs, ramps, balconies, canopies, and occasionally the structure, modelled the basic form of the new architecture.

Although structural discipline was part of the modern credo, the structure was usually subordinated to the form. This divergence between theory and practice confused the two main disciplines of the modern movement. Such architects as Le Corbusier expounded an apparent functionalism but at the same time expected the inspiration of the creative genius. Functionalists such as Stam who denied this need had sufficient taste to create equally accomplished buildings. For regardless whether his aesthetics were explicit or implicit, the modern architect went through the same design process in which functional analysis and economical assumptions were tempered by an a priori formalistic solution.* The architect wanted his architecture to grow naturally from the needs and resources of his time but he also wanted it to look like the art he had matured with. With the liberation of painting and sculpture from subject matter and architecture from the literalism of style, design encompassed the whole range of visual phenomena. From graphics through furniture to architecture and city planning, the visual designer ranged freely within the supposed objectivity of twentieth century scientific perception.

The architectural revolution celebrated at the Weissenhof exhibition by Continental architects was generally repudiated in Britain. The attitude of the conventional majority was summed up later by Sir Reginald Blomfield who was one of their most articulate spokesmen:

> [The new architecture] is essentially Continental in its origin and inspiration, and it claims as a merit that it is cosmopolitan. As an Englishman and proud of his country, I detest and despise cosmopolitanism.[1]

The reputable *The Architectural Review*, under the editorship of W. G. Newton, illustrated conventional buildings in a traditional manner, setting the occasional article on a modern architect amongst its usual neo-Classical or decorative arts selection.†

*(Throughout this book, asterisks refer to footnotes, numbers to the list of references which begins on page 207). This similarity in practice between the formalistic and functionalistic approaches to modern architecture was perceptively discussed by Henry-Russell Hitchcock and Philip Johnson in *The International Style: Architecture since 1922*, New York 1932, except that the authors did not take sufficient account of the human need for sustaining myths where there is no other basis for action.

†From 1921–2 Newton was coeditor with his father Ernest Newton after which he assumed sole responsibility until 1927. A late example of his policy, if the usual editorial time lag is taken into consideration, is the special issue on houses in December 1928 where Le Corbusier contributed an article to a survey described thus: "Six years have passed since the publication of the last Domestic Number of the Review; perhaps a hundred since any Editor has been in a position to form a collection of English houses equal in quality to those shown here ... The houses which follow are ... arranged in a rough kind of chronological order according to the 'style' in which they are dressed, so that it is possible for the reader ... to gauge the extent to which tradition influences modern design. All the houses have, of course, been built recently, but the sequence through Tudor,

The French model is uncompromising, 'and as a whole it can hardly be followed here. It will not fit the profound sentiment for accommodation with the past, and it will not maintain the genial belief in the worth of the individual.[2]

It was left to the weekly *The Architect and Building News* to publicize the events that were taking place abroad and this was mainly achieved through the writings of Howard Robertson.

Finishing his studies at the École des Beaux Arts in 1913, Robertson was prevented by the First World War from joining the staff at the AA school of architecture in London where he had previously been a student. He took up his appointment in 1919 at the age of 31 and remained first as principal and then director until his resignation in 1935. With his friend F. R. Yerbury, the AA Secretary, as photographer, Robertson travelled around Europe and the U.S.A. publishing innumerable articles in *The Architect and Building News* and familiarizing British architects with contemporary foreign practice.

He was enthusiastic for anything new and had a catholicity of taste that included modern architecture. Robertson's interests derived from nineteenth century theory where the belief that architecture expressed the characteristics of an age was tempered by the awareness that each building type had its own expressive requirements. Previous periods had moulded their image into a single form dominating both society and architecture; the industrial revolution democratized construction and forced architecture upon buildings of no cultural value. Confronted by the diverse needs of the new urban centres, architects found a hierarchy of suitable images in the styles of the past. The early twentieth century theorist accepted the problem but rejected the historical solution. It was unthinkable that buildings as socially opposite as an hotel and a prison could have the same aesthetic expression yet it was obvious that modern techniques should not be covered by traditional motifs. The search was for a vocabulary of forms sufficiently broad to cope with any programmatic requirement of plan, material or structure which might be exploited in the realization of the specific character of the design. For each of his neo-historical styles, the nineteenth century architect had his set of

---

Jacobean, and Georgian to the modern experiments at Silver End, gives an historical note to the collection . . .".

The Exhibition of Decorative Arts that was held in Paris in 1925, and which contained Le Corbusier's Pavillon de l'Esprit Nouveau, was then renowned for its advanced styling. Shand's article on the exhibition in the *AA Journal*, XL, 1924, pp. 30–32, while not including Le Corbusier, refers to the participating architects as mainly belonging to the "modern school".

rules. When eclecticism broke up the unity of a composition into combinations of varying stylistic components, a new regulating theory had to be established. The architectural theorist looked back to the great styles and tried to find eternal principles beneath their passing formal manifestations which could be projected as the basic requirements of any new stylistic combinations. The specific Renaissance system was peeled away to uncover the concepts *proportion* and *scale*, the soaring lines of the Gothic disclosed the concept *expression*, successful designs in any age were seen to have *unity*. Freed by these common denominators, the man of taste could find his enjoyments in the unlimited range of effects made possible by awareness of the past and exploitation of the present. To illustrate a point of composition, Robertson would compare St. Peter's, Rome, with Wright's Imperial Hotel.[3] This simple acceptance of the new architecture was offensive to his contemporaries who regarded it as a threat to traditional standards. In an autobiographical article, Robertson recalled that

> Continuous 'reportage' on modern architecture had its inevitable repercussions. I was considered by some to exert an evil influence, and was once tackled… by the late Maurice Webb, at that time [1925–7] Chairman of the RIBA Board of Architectural Education. He accused me of pernicious and corrupting influence on the general body of students through publicising modern trends, and in that way of doing a disservice to the architectural profession.[4]

At the same time that he took up his appointment at the AA, Robertson had also gone into practice with John Murray Easton. Their first important building, the Royal Horticultural Society Exhibition Hall in London, was completed in 1928. Although responsibility for the design was Easton's, the building exemplifies Robertson's eclecticism. The hall interior is functional, simple and bold, magnificently lit by the stepped walls of glazing, the exterior of the entrance block is pseudo-Georgian and the architectural detail is in the decorative arts style. The building is in the line of development that includes Peter Behrens' design for the house New Ways in Northampton and that of Thomas Tait for a house in Silver End, Essex. Both Behrens' exteriors, completed in 1926, and Tait's, in the following year, are cubical with stuccoed brick walls but neither has any other characteristics of the new aesthetic.* Like Easton and Robertson's exhibition hall, these houses derived from a moderate

---

*Tait's Ideal Home concrete house exhibited in 1928 was described by John Gloag as resembling "Australian butter in bulk." (See "Conquests in concrete", AJ, LXVII, 1928, p. 377).

approach to contemporary design where all historical motifs were left off to reveal basic building geometry but little was transformed in the process. What remained was tasteful construction decorated with the currently fashionable ornamentation. This compromise was offensive to modern architects who wished to extend the stylistic interpretation of history into the present. If, as Robertson argued, medieval architecture came into being because medieval men were virile and energetic, then modern architecture existed because modern man was mechanized. If each culture produced its own inevitable style, then modern architecture was the one true style and all others were wrong. This narrowing down of what was permissible, where the employment of form, structure and materials was not controlled by the demands of the moment but by a priori metaphysical decisions, seemed unnecessary and doctrinaire to Robertson. He refused to accept a single modern style apparently forgetting his homogeneous societies of the past in favour of the heterogeneity of his own.

> What appears to have happened [Robertson wrote in a review of the Weissenhof exhibition] in the present phase of the advanced modernist movement is this, that its leaders have leaped ahead, and instead of supplying in their architectural expression something which supplies a response to what might be considered an even balance between new tendencies and established traditions, have presupposed a future development of a certain stamp, and have built accordingly. They have created their client of the future, and they are catering for him to-day. This client is not, however, a totally imaginary being; he exists in certain numbers, but as yet is in a minority, and his type may either be modified, become extinct, or multiply exceedingly. But until he becomes much more averagely representative of the present-day citizen, the special architecture which caters to his taste will find more antagonists than backers.[5]

Modern architects did not share his qualms. "A great epoch has begun. There exists a new spirit." In 1927 Le Corbusier's *Vers une Architecture* was translated into English by Frederick Etchells and a theoretical basis was provided for the new architecture.[6]

> The French Modernists [wrote P. M. Stratton in *The Architectural Review*] have made so great an impression in England with their new impulse that there must surely have been room for their ideas. It is a dubious compliment to two nations to say their argument has rushed like wind into a vacuum; but at least Le Corbusier's book in Mr. Etchells' spirited translation has raised a storm. On a people so

essentially poetic and literary as the English the book has had a much more disturbing effect than the actual experiments of Lurçat, Le Corbusier et Jeanneret, and Mallet-Stevens.[7]

With the assuredness of his own ability, Le Corbusier set down how the new architecture was to be created. Starting with specific admonitions on the use of primary forms, his concrete images were supported by mathematical metaphors where visual rhythms resounded in man by an organic inevitability. Mixing mysticism with practical achievement, Le Corbusier's writing was necessarily ambiguous and could have meaning at different levels of complexity. So the architect was told that the plan was the generator. To Le Corbusier, such a plan was like a seed in which the finished form is predetermined. It was the synecdochic notation of a completed building. But this was not the meaning of plan in its normal architectural usage where it was often simply an agglomeration of rooms and circulation space. For many practical architects such a plan preceded the elevation of the walls and the door and window treatment of the facades. It was the simplest sequence in which to design a building. To be told to start with the plan was to be promised success by doing the obvious. "The 'styles' are a lie." "Economic law inevitably governs our acts and our thoughts." "Geometry is the language of man." Le Corbusier's maxims stripped of larger meaning provided his readers with a simple stereotype. *machines are alienating*

> M. Le Corbusier's chief point [commented *The Times Literary Supplement*] is that a house should be a machine for living in. The beauty of a machine depends on mathematical laws, and these laws should also guide the architect . . . The architect should therefore learn from the engineer; and M. Le Corbusier's book is an interesting and vigorous treatise on the application of engineering and mathematics to architecture.[8]

If the looseness of his writing permitted a superficial interpretation, its emotional declarations expressed the dignity of architecture as a mission. In the tradition of the Renaissance, the architect was no longer just a competent craftsman but was filled with the divine gifts of the creator. Le Corbusier's talent was matched by his pride, and this egocentricity penetrated his writing to vicariously elevate the reader.

> [The author, wrote the reviewer in *The Architect and Building News*] has that rare combination, vision coupled with spiritual insight. That is, he can pierce through the envelopes and trappings to the underlying idea, he knows and says that architecture is more than an en-

lightened utilitarianism; he insists upon the vital creative spark that shall lift the architect above the merely practical man and give his work permanence, for true permanence has nothing to do with materialism and the endurance of purely material things—it is essentially of the spirit.[9]

The architect became the builder of cities, the interpreter of an age, the leader of leaders. Writer, painter, sculptor, architect, planner; intellectual and aesthete; Le Corbusier personified a new millenium.

His attack on the neo-Classical was coupled with an appeal to the Classical past; his aim was to modernize traditional disciplines. While his tone was aggressive, his statements were not really offensive to Beaux Arts values. He condemned the Gothic because it lacked form while proving that the facade of Notre Dame in Paris was proportioned by an elementary geometry. He expounded another single style again based upon an explicit geometrical system. The twentieth century traditionalists had stripped down neo-Classicism to its underlying prism: Le Corbusier changed its rules and recast the form into a relevant symbol.

It will be interesting [wrote Harold Tomlison in *The Architects' Journal*] to watch the effects of the translation on our schools of architecture. Of late, even in this country, students have begun to show their dislike for the dreary routine of the "Orders", and are suspicious of the threadbare statement of their teachers that "The Orders are the only means of learning proportion". It is not unnaturally suspected that "The Orders are all we know" would be nearer to the truth. "Why", says the student, "when you have a perfectly good building, cover it up with that muck?"[10]

The aspiring modern architect with a Beaux Arts training, wishing to obey Le Corbusier's exhortations, had no need to change his method but only his formula. From the opposite direction Robertson's pragmatic approach resulted in an equivocal conclusion that made this route to a new architecture more difficult to follow. Robertson insisted upon an extensive diversified vocabulary of elements controlled by an equally flexible theory of architectural composition. New elements derived from program analysis fused imperfectly with those that continued to be acceptable; each design was individual with no general application. This eclectic indecision was swept away by Le Corbusier who substituted the simple image of a new universal Style.

In 1927 only seven British schools of architecture had full RIBA recognition. Of these the largest and most progressive were at the AA and Liverpool. The Liverpool school under Charles Reilly derived its reputation largely from his American enthusiasms and contacts which permitted his students to have six months practice in American offices without noticeably affecting their conventional training.[11] At the AA, Robertson's lectures on architectural composition excited his students while failing to free them from academic imitation. But change was rife. When the AA President, Gilbert H. Jenkins, virulently attacked the Weissenhof exhibition during his address at its general meeting in 1927, saying:

> A French exponent of modernism has built a plate glass box to form one of these new abodes—one could not conceive it as a home for anyone save a vegetarian bacteriologist.[12]

R. A. Duncan, who lectured on mediaeval architecture at the school, exclaimed that "if he were to take Mr. Jenkins' view, he would commit suicide".[13]

2 FIRST MOVEMENT

One has dreamed of the ultra-modern house in England. "Will they ever build homes like that in our countryside?" "Of course it's all right for France." "English clients would never tolerate these ultra-modern houses." And yet here it is, or about to be. The blow is falling; prepare to meet the shock! We wake up to find, not a newspaper account of an event, but a picture. The modern-house-in-the-English-countryside has arrived—at least its portrait—overnight. And a very good portrait it is, drawn by the artist himself, Mr. A. D. Connell.[14]

Robertson, in *The Architect and Building News*, was enthusing over the first ostensible example of modern architecture in Britain, the house High and Over, built in 1930. Amyas Connell was a New Zealander who, after completing his office training, had gone to England in 1924 with his friend Basil Ward. In London they worked as architectural assistants and joined the atelier of the University school of architecture where postgraduate students could obtain informal tuition. In 1926 they entered for the Rome Scholarship producing neo-Classical designs for a Royal Naval College: Connell was placed first and awarded the three year scholarship to study in Rome; Ward was placed second and given a special one year studentship. Towards the end of his second year in the British School at Rome, when he was twenty-seven years old, Connell received his first building commission from the retiring director, the archaeologist Bernard Ashmole, who wished to build himself a house and develop a thirteen acre site in Amersham near London. Returning to London at the beginning of 1929, Connell completed the designs by the middle of the year.

Even though the Y shaped plan of High and Over is novel, its interior spatial development is traditional in its static clustering of separate volumes. What is new for Britain is the treatment of its form: the angular shapes, the plane surfaces, the surface windows, the hovering

22

roof slab, the glazed staircase; these are all motifs derived from Continental practice. Yet while they are used coherently, they lack a motivating conceptual basis. The exterior of the house has a dynamic asymmetry that is of a different order to the symmetry of the interior. The large windows open up views and let in light but the spaces remain conventional rooms. This residue traditionalism can also be seen in the original landscaping which was designed by Connell though later modified by his client. There, the axes of the house were continued in neo-Classical star patterns that largely ignored the contours of the site.

The exterior form is a modern sheath over an essentially pre-modern dwelling. Connell, like many of the pioneer modern architects, came through the Classical tradition with the nineteenth century belief that true architecture is a direct stylistic expression of an age. As the Pantheon is to Rome and St. Peter's to the Renaissance, so modern architecture is to modern times. For the Classicist, modern architecture was part of a logical historical sequence but in physical design, the Classical tradition was stylistically a handicap, for a contemporary discipline was not just a matter of avoiding obsolete motifs but also of transforming the rules of composition. The Renaissance architect could unself-consciously cloak an irregular interior with the symmetry of his facade because his idea of beauty was greater than the commonsense requirements of his building program. The modern architect could take equal liberties with what was reasonable but his were of a different illogic. When Connell failed to make the exterior form a direct expression of the interior spaces, he had not yet completely grasped the new rules of quasi-functionalism.

On the other hand, Connell's treatment of the form of the building is almost an illustration of those principles of the type of architecture that was later popularized as the International Style. Construction is of a concrete frame, subtly modulating the facades, with a brick infill, both covered into a volume with a whitewashed stucco. Plate glass in steel frames continues and dematerializes the surface, producing a horizontal and vertical counterpoint. The service wing with its single-storey kitchen extension spoils the easterly compositions but the main garden elevation is masterly with its horizontal voids balanced by the bay window to the south and the tripartite vertical division of void, solid and canopy held by the proportioning of the structural mullions.

The facades [wrote Christopher Hussey in *Country Life*] being based on so balanced a plan and conceived in terms of mass and plane, can ignore symmetry of fenestration. The irregular placing of the voids is, indeed, a relief to the severity of the masses, forming a pattern at first sight wilful, but, on examination, subtle and logical.[15]

Modern architecture in Europe was greatly influenced by the Classical tradition and could easily appear to be a dialectical adaptation of it but, under the influence of nonobjective art, a mutation had taken place in the core of its aesthetic purpose. High and Over lacked the synthesis that had been attained by the major architects at the Weissenhof exhibition but in its originality provided a potent new image for Britain.

Connell's second house had no such ambiguity. New Farm, near Haslemere, Surrey, was built in 1932.

> The reader [commented *The Architect and Building News*] will hardly need to be told that this house is by the architect of Professor Ashmole's celebrated—some might say "notorious"—house, "High and Over", at Amersham. "High and Over" startled the architectural profession by brilliantly demonstrating that current notions of domestic planning and design were somewhat rusty.[16]

New Farm has an ingenious fan shaped plan with the service neck opening out into a spread of living and bedrooms facing in a southerly direction. The form, or integrated forms, of the house grow easily and interestingly from the inner spaces which develop from a hall, reached at the ground floor level along a turning narrow entrance corridor and opening back into a glass walled staircase whose roof moves forward again to lightly cap the serrated block below.

> At first sight [continued *The Architect and Building News*] the plan appears capricious. The shapes are unfamiliar, though the main circulations are conventional. But on examination each apparent oddity is found to be based on sound reasoning. And, curiously enough, these odd shapes and odder fenestration group into a whole which, though it has its surprises, is consistent and harmonious. Mr. Connell has realized the freedom which reinforced concrete constructions can give—the *plan libre* of Le Corbusier—and he is not afraid of novelty.[17]

The design is a tour de force that has none of the aesthetic contradictions of the previous house. While the hall is centred on the axis of the main sector, this has no visual significance within the interior sequence. Like the work of one section of the modern movement, the rooms themselves have little spatial interest especially as the structural grid appears unpleasantly in all the major spaces. The interest derives from the juxtaposition of light and view, the outward looking southern rooms being backed by a spine of western sun. This growth of plan achieves its climax externally in the elegant solution of its difficult geometry. Slotted screen walls, cantilevered canopy and internal staircase, angular windows and roof deck railings were brought together in the entrance approach to achieve one of the most evocative modern images to be produced in England.

By this time there were other modern buildings. The Royal Corinthian Yacht Club at Burnham-on-Crouch, Essex, designed by Joseph Emberton, was completed in 1931. The club's simple functional planning, its bold massing of glass and cement (covering a structure of steel with brick infill), and the nautical air of its stepped cantilevered floors, produced a sophisticated example of the International Style that, with High and Over, was England's contribution to the exhibition that inaugurated the architectural department of New York's Museum of Modern Art in 1932.[18] Emberton, who was born in 1890 and trained at the Royal College of Art, had practised on his own since 1926 and had achieved recognition with the massive Empire Hall at the Olympic Exhibition site in London. After Universal House, a London office building, built in 1934 with horizontal bands of clear and opaque glass, his work had a forceful individuality and, while he was associated with the MARS group during the following decade, this together with his lack of ideological intensity, kept him apart from his younger colleagues.

Another early practitioner of modern architecture of this generation was Owen Williams who, also born in 1890, had already been knighted for his work as engineering consultant to the 1924 British Empire Exhibition. Trained as an engineer, he decided at the end of the nineteen twenties to combine practice as an architect, and his design for the Boots factory, Nottingham in 1931, a reinforced concrete mushroom structure with a seven hundred feet long front facade of glass, was widely admired as a model of functionalism. His reputation declined as his later designs became architecturally more pretentious yet if his design for a synagogue, built in 1938, was unacceptable, the 1935 Pioneer Health Centre in London was another landmark in the British modern movement. Not only was the Centre's program a novel experiment in social health but the building's glass and concrete structure exemplified its contemporary purpose and was a vigorous statement of one branch of the new style. Nevertheless Williams, even more than Emberton, was never accepted as an equal by his later contemporaries who, with their greater metaphysical involvement with aesthetics, continued to regard him as an interesting engineer.

A third architect of this period was George Checkley, a Liverpool graduate from New Zealand. His first house in Cambridge, where he taught, was completed in 1931, a rigidly symmetrical composition covering a conventional interior; his second, Thurso House, had a more developed interior space and a strikingly composed garden facade. But with his appointment to the Polytechnic in London, Checkley essentially gave up practice.

The failure of these modern architects to remain influential left Connell alone as a continuing celebrity, not only for the quality of his work but also for the controversy it caused. Emberton's first design for the Yacht Club was shown at the Royal Academy: Connell, however, from the beginning, was subjected to the animosity of his more conventional colleagues.

Amongst the powers given to local authorities by the Town and Country Planning Act of 1932 were those permitting the regulation of the size, height, design and external appearance of buildings and the rejection of any projected building that would be "likely seriously to injure the amenity of the locality." The aim of these provisions was to prevent unsightly and sporadic development but conservative lay committees used this part of the act to protect their communities from the encroachment of modern architecture. To aid local authorities in their decisions, the RIBA in conjunction with the Council for the Preservation of Rural England had already set up an architects' panel system, a voluntary organization within the provincial Allied Societies. Originally including other interests, these panels were narrowed to a sub-panel of three architects in response to the need for quick decisions on elevational control. If the design were rejected, the intending builder could appeal to the Minister of Health who was entitled to ask the RIBA president to send an arbitrator.[19] At High and Over where a similar, pre-1932 Act, amenity requirement had prevailed, Connell and his client had been held up over the disputed design of the water tower and were only permitted on appeal to proceed after hearing that

> When the plans came before the Committee . . . a great many of the members were startled, and with extreme reluctance, the plans were passed. If this matter had been confined entirely to the house and its immediate appurtenances the Committee felt that they would make the best of it, but when the water tower was submitted, they felt still greater reluctance to acquiesce. The general feeling of the Committee was that the design was ultra-modern, and therefore a certain amount of opposition must be expected . . .[20]

On the next occasion that Connell was involved in a design appeal, the resultant action was more acrimonious.

Ward, who after his year in Rome had been in Burma for three years during which time he had married Connell's sister, returned to go into partnership with him and in 1933 they submitted a design for a pair of semi-detached houses to be located at Ruislip, Middlesex. As a matter of coincidence, the Ruislip-Northwood Urban District Council had been the initiator of architectural control in Britain having enacted such a provision in 1914. Invoking their town planning scheme and the support of the Ruislip Architects' Panel, the council turned down the proposed design.

> The Council [reported the Panel] no doubt already realizes that this is not an ignorant, but a consciously modern, design which, in external form, is deliberately odd. We see nothing in the planning which would render it necessary that it should be treated in this fashion which is not new but of Continental origin. We are satisfied that, despite full publicity for all discoverable examples in the technical Press, there is in fact little work of this character being built in this country and if, as appears likely, it becomes unfashionable the isolated examples are likely to prove unacceptable to tenants and may even become derelict, to the disadvantage of surrounding property . . . Architects might be interested to see these designs carried out, but we conceive it to be the duty of elected representatives to have some regard to the feelings and wishes of the community which they represent and, in our opinion, nine out of ten of the Ruislip population would view these houses in their proposed situation with active disfavour.[21]

Called upon to arbitrate, the RIBA nominee upheld that "the said plans sections or elevations are in the matter of design injurious to the amenity of the neighbourhood".[22] Thus both local and national representatives of the profession publicly reprimanded two of their colleagues for designing a building that was not in keeping with its place in the community.

> The Panel system [commented a leader in *The Architects' Journal*] was not instituted as machinery for the public exhibition of private disagreement among architects on aesthetic questions, but in order to compel aesthetic considerations to be given to building enterprises in which the architect has no voice whatever; nor was the Institute founded to arbitrate on aesthetic matters between different factions among its own membership . . . If the Institute allows its more reactionary members to obstruct the enterprise of its more progressive members, the next stage will be even more harmful to the Institute's authority. The younger men, the future backbone of the profession,

will be forced to organize themselves into a defensive *bloc*; and that *bloc*, if the same state of things continues, will eventually be forced to retreat from the RIBA altogether.[23]

From Ruislip onwards, the modern architect expected to be victimized by reactionary forces and to have one's designs rejected was part of the price of belonging to the avant-garde. As it turned out, after some months of negotiations, the design by Connell and Ward was approved with only slight modifications and a further building by them on an adjoining site was passed by the same council without objection. But the battle was joined. Like Le Corbusier, the British modern architects did not intend to be nonconformists but, forced into this position by a conservative society, they took pride in their social ostracism. Writing over twenty years later, Maxwell Fry recalled that

> A house in the Chilterns by Connell and Ward drew some of the first fire from an outraged public and it was not before we had been turned off three sites and found one sufficiently remote that I was able to build my first house,* and with the limitation imposed by the local council that traditional materials should be employed.[24]

In 1933, Connell and Ward were joined in partnership by Colin Lucas. Born in London and trained at the Cambridge University school of architecture, Lucas had formed his own building firm and at twenty-four years of age, in 1930, built the first monolithic reinforced concrete house in Britain. Noah's House, in Bourne End, Buckinghamshire, designed for his father, has little architectural grace; his own house The Hopfield, built in 1933 near Wrotham, Kent, achieves an interesting form within its very small size but is of little consequence. During the rest of the decade, however, the partnership, continuing the standard set by Connell, produced a series of the finest houses in Britain. But while their reputation is based on the quality of their work, it also derives from the controversy that began and continued to be centered around them.[25]

While the first modern buildings were being built, the Architectural Press in London, under the twenty-five year old Hubert de Cronin Hastings, was modernizing its editorial policy. Initially the new literary movement was more dull than serious. The young future modern architects, Maxwell Fry and Raymond McGrath, started in 1927 to

*Fry meant his first house in the *modern* style at Chipperfield, Hertfordshire, designed in 1934. Other house designs rejected during this period were by McGrath, Tecton and Chermayeff.

publish articles in *The Architects' Journal* that were reactionary and trivial. The future modern critic, Morton Shand, began his contributions a year earlier with "Wine-cellar design in the private house".[26]

Fry had graduated from Liverpool University in 1923 and gone south to work in London. McGrath, an Australian, had graduated in 1926 from the University of Sydney and a travelling fellowship took him to Cambridge University where he became its first research student in architecture. Shand, who was older than the others—he was a contemporary (and cousin) of Robertson—was educated at Eton and Cambridge and at the Sorbonne. After serving in the First World War, he settled in France. Although he was invited to write articles for the Architectural Press, his real interest in the nineteen-twenties was the five books he wrote on food and wine. Initially his taste in architecture was for the decorative; he overpraised Roux-Spitz and Mallet-Stevens and overlooked Le Corbusier.* But his involvement with architectural journalism brought him into contact with many European architects and by the end of the decade he wrote with authority.

[Sweden has] refused to behave like the "gifted and promising young artist" who, having painted the picture of the year in 1923, and repeated his success in the Salon of 1925, can be relied on to produce copies of these masterpieces season by season until at forty-five he is sterilized into immortality with an RA admission. England, of course, is more puzzled by this gratuitous flouting of an established reputation than nations less wedded to changelessness, because England is still busily turning out Adam plasterwork, Wedgewood china and Chippendale chairs, which are faithful to their eighteenth-century models in all except finish, without any disturbing suspicion that the time for period reproductions may be drawing to a precipitate and (commercially) rather disastrous close. Odd fellows, these Swedes, looking a gift horse in the mouth like that! No proper business instincts! Just when they had started to build up a nice little novelty trade in stylish High Art lines—real high-class fancy goods, natty but not too jazzy—they go and change the management, write off their old stock and start on something the travellers had never as much as seen. Ostberg was the man who put it across for them and collared the gold medals. Well, now, here's the new boss, Asplund, gone clean balmy.[27]

*Shand's judgments can be compared with those of the young American architectural historian Henry-Russell Hitchcock in his book *Modern Architecture: Romanticism and Reintegration*, New York 1929, p. 174: "Where at Boulogne-sur-Seine a villa of Mallet-Stevens stands beside the Cook house of Le Corbusier, the inferiority of the former is startlingly revealed to the most casual observer."

Reporting in *The Architectural Review* on the 1930 Stockholm Exhibition, Shand came close to the orthodox modern dogma though whereas most modern architects would have insisted that the discipline of functionalism preceded or dispensed with the delights of formalism, Shand was more interested in the appearance of things than in their underlying rationalizations.

> It may as well be candidly admitted that we erect mechanist buildings, not because we must but because we like them ... Mechanism may be the whim of the moment, but that does not alter the patent fact that there is more to be said for it than for any other. It is the only "style" which does not oblige its exponents to have recourse to insincerity or shams when faced with the problem of housing a motor-boat or motor-car, an aeroplane or a locomotive ... The present age finds the shape of steamers, aircraft, cooking ovens, turbines, transmission poles and silos so infinitely more beautiful than traditional art forms ...[28]

Like the Weissenhof model suburb, the Stockholm Exhibition created a microcosm of a novel world; of simple, light volumes and plane surfaces delineated in steel and glass. Sunshades flapping and flags flying, the new aesthetic was brought to Scandinavia with all the authority of its architect, Gunnar Asplund, one of Europe's leading neo-Classicists. Modern architecture was respectable. Shand, who two years earlier had written of Easton and Robertson's horticultural hall that it was "hard to moderate one's enthusiasm for this *débonnaire* young building",[29] narrowed his definition of the new aesthetic.

> For the 1930 Stockholm Exhibition has at least taught us that the future of the machine as an integral organ of modern culture is assured; and that its technical perfection as an art-form is only a matter of time. In it there lies the germ of an Augustan architecture magnificent enough to satisfy both the conditions and the aspirations of a great, a golden age, and worthy of man's ultimate enfranchisement from the tyranny and the superstitious terrors of his own timid and hide-bound imagination.[30]

About the same time, *The Architectural Review* promoted a competition for the interior design of two rooms for "Lord Benbow". Being a Clydeside shipbuilder, he had become "intimately acquainted with the school of thought now associated with the name of C. R. Mackintosh. This early enthusiasm has gradually crystallized into a devotion for the later developments of the modern movement and has led him to seek for a distinguished modern treatment in the decoration of his apartments."[31]

However, he was not obsessively modern. He found abstract patterns loathsome and wished to have sporting objects incorporated into the basic decor. The editor of *The Architectural Review*, in his report as assessor of the competition, defined the meaning of the word "modern".

> It cannot be defined positively as metal furniture and the Corbusier aesthetic, nor negatively as absence of traditional feeling. In the last extremity words like "modern" have to be boiled down into something quite simple, and in the assessor's mind they boiled themselves down to this: that as decoration is regarded by the modern mind as architecture, and as architecture is regarded as involving, first and foremost, the imaginative exploitation of the plan conceived three-dimensionally or plastically, so a decorative scheme conceived in a modern way should exploit the idiosyncrasies native to the plan—and exploit them in such a way that one would be nearly justified in saying that the plan dictated the scheme of decoration. In other words, "expression of plan" is a governing factor inside as well as outside a piece of architecture. The plan as it develops three-dimensionally suggests the basis of its own decorative interpretation.[32]

The idea that art is in any way inevitable has more appeal to the non-creative person than to the practising architect who must construct something where there is nothing. It is one thing for posterity to perceive a style as emanating from the spirit of an age and another for those involved at the time to produce a style that does emanate from the spirit of that age. All artifacts reflect the time of their manufacture but some have more or less significance for people at contemporary or later periods. Those who argued that architects should act as midwives letting the building program give birth to the design so that the result would inevitably be evocative to the society that generated both problem and solution, made architecture appear as a matter of common sense. But for the majority it was easier to follow someone who told you what to do than those who stated that whatever you did was good so long as you did it unselfconsciously. The architect, faced with the decision whether to place a window here or there, preferred a copybook to the uncertainty of letting the window decide for itself.

The most cultured of the architectural magazines of the period, *The Architectural Review* was beautifully laid out, its special issues were intelligent and forcibly presented, its industrial design articles were stimulating and its departmental comments against architectural vandalism were always clever. Its editorial selection of buildings, however, showed a superficiality of taste that uncritically gave a wide range of designs of varying quality equally fine graphic presentation.* Neverthe-less the support given by such a reputable magazine, together with that of its affiliated publication *The Architects' Journal*, was decisive propa-ganda for the converging group of modern architects.

The first prize for Lord Benbow's apartment was won by McGrath. At Cambridge, where his research project had been on the development of the theatre, McGrath had renovated a Victorian house with the exotic use of glass and whimsical decoration. His client, Mansfield Forbes, a member of the Faculty of Fine Arts and Architecture at the university, had an enthusiasm for bringing people of different talents together for their mutual stimulation and his house Finella became a gathering place for young architects. There McGrath, Serge Chermayeff and Wells Coates met Valentine Goldsmith, a director of the British Broadcasting Corporation and when it occupied new premises in London, the three were invited to design a number of its interiors under McGrath's direction.

Coates was already known for his work as a designer. Born in Japan, educated in Canada with an engineering doctorate from London University, after a period of travelling he began his career in 1927 at the age of thirty-four when he was invited to Cornwall by the firm of Crysede. His first completed shop in Cambridge the following year not being to the liking of one of the partners, Coates returned to the London area where he worked for the other partner and the new firm of Cresta. In 1931, with Chermayeff and Fry amongst the runners-up, he won the competition for an exhibition stand organized by the Venesta plywood company which had used Le Corbusier, Jeanneret and Perriand the year before and was trying to popularize its product through the enlightened publicity of Jack Pritchard.

The BBC interiors were published in *The Architectural Review* in 1932. The same year, F. R. S. Yorke started writing for the magazine, Berthold Lubetkin contributed to a special issue on Russia, and an article by Shand was illustrated by the work of his protégés. The Architectural Press had become the new group's centre.

Robertson's pragmatism had been superseded. The forms of modern architecture had been established and modern architects knew what to do. The eclectics did not and their indecision was pushed aside by the

*As examples: the August 1931 issue includes the jazzy Malmaison Restaurant, the neo-Corinthian head offices for Lloyds Bank and the eclectic Whitgift Grammar School. Or—the March 1935 issue on modern houses ranges from the good (by Chitty and Tecton) through the mediocre (by Chermayeff) to the bad (by Smith).

dogma of their antagonists. It might, Michael Dugdale, an AA graduate, wrote in *The Architectural Review* discussing *Modern Architectural Design* published in 1932, "have been no loss, but some gain, if Mr. Robertson had come forward with an axe to grind, instead of so ostentatiously with none".[33] His colleague, Duncan, was more explicit.

The book as a whole [he wrote in *The Architects' Journal*] is an exposition of the 1925 attitude which was closely associated with handicraftsmanship, although it seeks to throw off the fetters of traditional formulae. No very clear dividing line is drawn between the work of men like Wright, Dudok and Höger, and say, Gropius, Corbusier and van Rohe. It is, perhaps, impossible to put men into watertight compartments, but it becomes almost daily more obvious that there are* distinct categories of modernists, though many intermediate shades of opinion lie between. The former category, of which perhaps Höger's work is a good example, consists of highly individualist designers still closely identified with traditional materials and methods. Work in the second category—that of van Rohe for example—represents a very much more violent change, and is primarily concerned with the maximum exploitation of modern industrial methods and products for building, as well as quasi-scientific organization and planning. But this is not all, for perhaps the most important aspect of the work of this latter school is that it embodies an attempt to produce an harmonious setting for a completely mechanical age, a setting in which such things as the aeroplane and the motorbus would not appear incongruous. There is already a marked cleavage between the two groups, and this is likely in the near future to develop into another battle of the styles. Without discussing the rights and wrongs of the matter, it is obvious that the adherents of the "Craftsmanship" school will receive support from the existing conditions of the building trades and a public which likes something new, but not too new, and certainly not a shock. Its chief recommendation will lie not so much in logic as in humanism, and the fact that such architecture can, at a pinch, be incorporated into an existing setting, for it is not entirely devoid of the link of associated ideas. The advanced group, on the other hand, is supported by the march of events in science and industry as a whole, and a general economic tendency towards the elimination of handicraftsmanship, which ultimately entails the substitution of other materials for brick, stone and wood, or at any rate as far as their traditional use is concerned, for only

*The original reads "there are no distinct categories" which is obviously an error.

33

materials readily adapted to factory processes will be employed. These factors will lend powerful unconscious support to drastic innovation.[34]

In Britain, Duncan's first category included the work of the London Passenger Transport Board which in association with Adams, Holden and Pearson were producing a number of suburban underground stations in a brick idiom reminiscent of the Dutchman Willem Dudok.[35] The first of these new-style buildings (superseding a previous series faced in Portland stone) were erected along the Arnos Grove extension line which opened in the summer of 1932.* But these had no influence on the accelerating intransigency.

While the British had no national representation at the Congrès Internationaux d'Architecture Moderne which had been founded in 1928 with Sigfried Giedion as secretary, Robertson had been accepted as a delegate to their meetings in Frankfurt and Brussels. The next meeting was scheduled for 1933 by which time Robertson had been overtaken by the British avant-garde. Advised by Shand, Giedion wrote directly to Coates whose friendship embraced diverse personalities.

> To our great regret [he wrote] no English group of the Congresses has been formed. Mr. Robertson and some of his friends attended our Brussels Congress, but they afterwards informed us that no interest in our movement existed in England . . . Please let us know if interest in the new architecture is still so lukewarm in England, and whether there are really no young men to be found there who have the courage, and feel it their duty, to form a collective organisation, and establish contact with us?[36]

In April 1933 the loose heterogeneous alliance of British progressive designers and architects was replaced by the Modern Architectural Research Group (MARS)† with Coates as chairman debarring Robertson amongst others for being insufficiently modern or too decorative.

*Another public authority which produced a series of Dudok-type buildings was the Miners' Welfare Committee with its Liverpool educated architect J. H. Forshaw. These pithead baths, however, only began to be completed in 1933 and while illustrations of the finished buildings were included in the *Miners' Welfare Fund 12th. Report* 1933, published in 1934, they were neither readily accessible nor widely publicized until later.

†The original members of the MARS group appear to have been Coates, Fry (vice-chairman), Yorke (secretary), Pleydell-Bouverie, Connell, Ward, Lucas, Samuel, Skinner, Betjeman, Shand, Hastings, Gloag with Lubetkin, Sweett and Boumphrey joining soon afterwards. See F. H. Elgohary, *Wells Coates, and his position in the beginning of the modern movement in England*, unpublished doctoral thesis, London University 1966.

The Group is made up of modern architects and allied technicians [wrote *The Architects' Journal* later summarizing its aims] who have been willing to profit by those experiments in form and function which were worked out almost simultaneously in many countries during the last quarter of a century and which have produced a modern style both rational in character and international in distribution, and to assume some of the architect's social responsibilities. The Group has been formed primarily for research, which, within the terms of the task the members have set themselves, includes not only technical investigations into purely architectural matters such as planning and structure, but also includes rather deep probings into the whole structure of society.[37]

For the next meeting of CIAM which took place in July to analyze the problems of the functional city, the congress sailed through the Mediterranean, Coates as the senior British delegate, to compose the manifesto known as the Athens Charter. The meeting was to have been held in Moscow but had been indefinitely postponed by its Soviet sponsors.

3 FOREIGN AFFAIRS

In the popular view, revolutionary art and revolutionary politics were related social manifestations. The nineteenth century developed the concept that art is organically connected with society; Marxism included art in the ideological superstructure of any given economic system. When the Communist revolution took place in Russia, it seemed inevitable that a new art would be born. The futurists at first assumed that they would be its cultural expression but having grown out of the old Russia where they had, by necessity, been of the bohemian fringe, they soon gave way to the constructivists who, in a theoretically classless society which had no place for alienated egoists, proclaimed an objectivity derived from the same logic as the workers' machines.

Initially the politicians could not make up their minds as to which style of art would most aptly portray a Communist society. Lenin favoured an eclectic selection from the best of the past believing that there was nothing necessarily advantageous in artistic novelty. He thought experimentation inevitable in the search for a beauty that was not to be seen in the various contemporary styles. In the year of his death, the artist's right to work without political restraint was embodied in a resolution of the Political Bureau of the Communist Party which refused to propound a party style observing that revolutionists, having ruthlessly destroyed the existing order, could now be more tolerant towards other views: proletarian art, although preferred, would have to compete freely with academic and progressive art for public acceptance. In literature, this aloofness lasted until all writers were united into a single union; in architecture, the change came with the competition for the Palace of the Soviets.

Stalin's ideal of Socialism in one country required a nationalistic popular culture. In 1932 the squabblings of the various art factions were ended when the government disbanded them. Even the workers' organizations were considered subversive as they not only claimed to represent the revolution but also believed themselves to be an autonomous part of it. This self-sufficiency was entirely unacceptable to the politicians who considered art as a function of political action. By a resolution of the Central Committee of the Communist Party, all writers who claimed to support the USSR were ordered into a single union under political domination. The other art organizations were similarly reorganized, in 1933 the Union of Soviet Architects replacing a mêlée of architectural groups.

To the Western observer, this detailed manoeuvring was lost in the general activity of Soviet reconstruction. In the mythology of modern architecture, Soviet architecture was logically in the International Style. As a representative of the New Fabian Research Bureau had reported on his fact-finding visit, it was international, revolutionary, industrial, economical.[38] The USSR was modern architecture's habitat. Such a simplified view foundered with the competition for the Palace of the Soviets. While nothing in Lubetkin's detailed description of formalist, functionalist and symbolist groups, published in *The Architectural Review*[39] for architects who intended to visit or work in the USSR, suggested the imminent reaction in architectural design, it was evident, as the magazine recognized, that the design of a Soviet palace was a turning point in the history of Soviet architecture. But given the popular analysis of the situation the result of the competition, where designs by Le Corbusier, Gropius and Mendelsohn were rejected in favour of the neo-Classical entry by the Russian Iofan, could only be seen as a temporary aberration which would automatically correct itself given time. Art expresses the spirit of the age; revolutionary politics produce revolutionary architecture.

The Soviet analysis was more realistic. Architects, involved with the subtleties of their own specialty had neglected the emotional needs of the people. Both formalism and functionalism were useful in promoting new techniques and disciplines but were only a means and not an end in themselves. The former led to an art that adulated the machine instead of the human being; the latter to a utilitarianism that denied that architecture was an art. The prospering Soviet worker needed a more opulent architecture that would symbolize the greatness of the society he had created. Challenged by the monumental demands of the Palace of the Soviets, modern architects failed to produce a design to match the popularity of the nearby Kremlin. Lenin's theory of eclecticism was vindicated.

To the Communists, Communism was the most advanced political conception of the time. Lenin spent much of his activity as a writer not just condemning the capitalism of the past but attacking alternative contemporary political solutions. The Western artist similarly believed that good art manifested the most advanced perceptions of the time and that modern architecture was the only valid architecture for the twentieth century. An age produced bad art when it portrayed the unimportant; it succeeded where it located those images which evoked awareness of the new significances. The nineteenth century apparently failed when its inhabitants lost the sensitivity either to produce or to respond to this degree of awareness. Materialism had dominated art which was no longer left to find its own extent of achievement but was circumscribed down to the common taste. The middle class had wanted an understand-able art and rejected the esoteric; the twentieth century condemned it for that. For a revolutionary society to want the same sort of art was inconceivable. When Lenin asked whether artists should give cake and sugar to a minority when the mass of workers lacked black bread, the artist could only assume that this was a temporary predicament while the people rediscovered their souls.

The founding group of CIAM had stated that they were putting architecture back on its real plane, the economic and social plane, and their first study was on the low cost house. Their aim, however, was not to represent the common man but to interpret him. Le Corbusier had no desire to be of the urban proletariat. It was his mission to house them as he diagnosed their needs. For himself, he was proudly of the intelli-gentsia. Art is essentially arrogant, he wrote, and performs its proper function when it addresses itself to the chosen few. While in Communist metaphysics the state would wither away, in progressive capitalism the enlightened minority would always be responsible for the relatively unenlightened majority. Architects of the nineteenth century had given the bourgeoisie what they wanted; the twentieth century architect was a man of sterner moral fibre bestowing upon the proletariat what their needs demanded.

The Russian futurists and constructivists had seen themselves as artistic shock troops symbolizing the revolution. The workers, however, were destined to satisfy their own tastes. They wanted their art to have immediate emotional relevance; the government regarded art as its propagandistic extension. Neither could accept a style whose major claim to merit was based on a future immortality. The modern artist, progeny of the fiasco of the nineteenth century movements, refused to gauge success by popular acceptance and looked to other generations to justify his work.

The enemy had been the bourgeoisie. With its overthrow the artist believed that natural innocence would once again unite art with taste.

The common man, throwing aside the superficialities of the *nouveau riche*, would respond to the truth of the artist's vision. Unaffected by the trappings of civilization, Soviet man would see life anew with the same pure sensitivity as the artist. With this naive hope of social rebirth, the modern architect was more sorrowful than angry when the USSR became artistically reactionary. Even Le Corbusier did not resort to his customary invective when his Palace of the Soviets project was declined, merely commenting that while he regretted its decision, the Soviet government was probably justified in selecting a less sophisticated design.[40]

At the same time that modern architecture was being rejected in its country of adoption, it was also being rejected in the country of its origin. Closely linked to the USA by American loans, the German economy had foundered with the American depression. With unemployment quadrupled and the Social Democratic party unable to agree on its relief, the chancellor resigned and the government became successively more reactionary. In January 1933, having rapidly grown from the smallest to the largest party in parliament, the National Socialists took over control under Hitler. *The Times*, reporting his accession, noted that while his personal magnetism was unquestionable, nothing was known of his administrative capacities. Within a few months all other political parties had been suppressed and the refugees were coming out of Germany.

The Nazi philosophy of art was similar to that generally prevailing in the rest of the Western world. Art reflects the spirit of a nation and great nations produce great works of art which, embodying their souls, give them immortality. The Egyptians are remembered for their pyramids, the Greeks for their temples. Art is not a minority entertainment but a collective expression of hope and faith portraying the beautiful and good as the goal of civilization. At this point the fanatical Nazi logic led to the denunciation of modern art. The converse axiom that bad people produce bad art proved that Jews and Communists were responsible for the contemporary art movements that titillated misfits with decadent images. If this overt declaration set them apart from those who thought similarly but did not say so, the remainder of their cultural program was quite exemplary. Lacking genius in those arts of music, painting and sculpture in which the German people had previously excelled, they would glorify themselves in the essential art of architecture. Hitler's recipe was conventional: Buildings should be practical, expressive of their function (a theatre ought to look like a theatre), and should conform to those eternal principles of composition embedded in the architecture of the past. Like the British majority, the Germans favoured the neo-Classical as a model and only differed in their choice of precedent. Buildings such as the Southampton Civic Centre and the Berlin Air Ministry, built at approximately the same time, have much in common except that the one was democratically chosen and the other dictatorially imposed. Yet as a social art, the Nazi approach to architecture had much that architects elsewhere could admire. The distinction demanded between private and public architecture, the one modest, the other monumental, was the accepted basis of civic design while insistence that it was the duty of the state to support the arts so that its cultural heritage would not die was most welcome at a time of economic depression. "Everywhere in Germany", wrote a detached observer, "one sees signs of a great building revival; the Third Reich is an architect's paradise".[41]

At first the British government was not alarmed by the Wall Street crash. Just over four months earlier the Labour party had formed its second minority government being, for the first time in its history, the largest party in parliament. With chronic unemployment as one of its major problems, a committee was set up to find a solution but as it deliberated, the situation worsened. The average ten percent unemployment rate of just over a million workers rose to fifteen percent in the year that followed. Frustrated by the ineptitude of the unemployment committee, one of its members, Sir Oswald Mosley, resigned and presented his own proposals for improving the situation. When these were rejected by the government, Mosley quit to start a new party of his own. By August 1931 the effects of the American depression had almost reduced Britain to bankruptcy. Faced with two million unemployed and British and foreign pressure to cut unemployment relief, the government split; the Labour prime minister with minority Labour support formed a coalition government with a Conservative majority. A few months later in a general election the Labour party was routed and the Conservatives again took office. The failure of the traditional parties to solve the overwhelming problem of unemployment that reached its peak in the summer of 1932 encouraged agitation for unorthodox action. Mosley, still trying to implement his economic proposals, gave up his attempt to gain a democratic following and launched his British Union of Fascists.

In his theory of a corporate state, the government was neither for capitalists nor workers but was made up of young men of action who would ensure the collaboration of all segments of the nation. Everyone would be given due representation through a system of occupational corporations. The Fascists, Mosley argued, able to plan rationally, would be capable of solving all economic problems. They would be impersonal social engineers making things work properly for the good of king and country. The British Union of Fascists for a time made a reasonable appeal to intellectuals faced with legislative paralysis, but soon took on peripheral characteristics that were part of an unacceptable foreign fanaticism. After Hitler's rise to power, brutality and anti-Semitism became integral components of Mosley's policy. At mass rallies the man who had written that the idea of dictatorship was foreign to the British character became the Leader of the Blackshirts denouncing Jewry and pausing purposefully while his thugs beat up dissenters.[42]

The depression in England had been less severe on the building trades than in the heavy industries. Overall construction only fell by twelve percent and the number of dwellings built by private enterprise remained around the pre-depression level. The construction of public and commercial buildings, however, fell by almost a third and these made up the most important part of architects' commissions.[43] By the end of 1931, the RIBA was expressing alarm.

> The unemployment in the architectural profession [stated the president in an appeal for funds] is rapidly reaching unprecedented dimensions. With the stoppage or postponement of municipal and private building, architectural assistants are being thrown out of work at short notice, and in many cases this is causing dire distress. It is difficult to obtain accurate figures, but we believe that by Christmas there will be a large number of architects out of work, and unless a great change takes place in the situation the appalling numbers which are reported from New York and elsewhere may well be approached.[44]

This did not happen. At its peak, the number of unemployed architects requesting help through the Architects' Unemployment Fund was little more than one hundred when there were seven thousand members of the RIBA and three thousand more in the Allied Societies.* By 1933, through its housing output, the building industry was out of its slump and quickly climbing to its pre-Second World War summit.

---

*These figures should be compared with those applying to the U.S.A. where overall private construction fell by 85 per cent. By 1932 in the New York region, 2551 persons had registered for relief with the Architects Emergency Committee. See "Unemployment relief measures", *Architectural Record*, LXXII, 1932, pp. 354–360.

The situation, however, was easily exploited to make a disproportionate outcry against the first refugees arriving from Germany.

At a time when so many of our young and vital architects are in a desperate position, [stated a Fascist Week article reprinted in *The Architects' Journal*] the Royal Institute of British Architects chooses to welcome alien architects and to encourage them in professional practice within this country . . . We have been affronted by the spectacle of prosperous British architects lavishing on these aliens, at big professional functions, encouragement which they conspicuously withhold from the younger architects of their own race . . .[45]

The Fascists were exaggerating. Unlike some of the other professions in Germany, that of architecture had few Jewish members. Furthermore the RIBA was quick to reinforce an already stringent immigration policy.

It has appeared to the Council that a misapprehension exists regarding the attitude of the RIBA towards the question of admitting foreign architects to practise in this country. This matter has received the serious consideration of the Council and in December last [1933] a letter was sent to the Ministry of Labour defining the Council's attitude. The following are extracts from the letter in question:—
"The Minister will be aware of the serious state of depression through which the building industry is still passing and the consequent lack of employment for architects at the present time, and while my Council feel it is for the Minister to consider whether the architectural profession should be treated in any way differently from any other profession or trade in regard to the admission of foreign architects to practise in this country, they are of opinion that the admission of foreign architects should be limited to those with special qualifications who are in a position to establish themselves in independent practice."[46]

Under these conditions probably only about a dozen* German refugee architects were admitted into Britain during the next three years but of these Erich Mendelsohn and Walter Gropius were internationally famous.

*According to the Institut für Zeitgeschichte, probably only about 3 percent of the Bund Deutscher Architekten at this time were Jews, that is about 75 members. Of course, not all architects were members of the BDA and not all refugees were Jews. The figure of twelve is based on the recollections of members of The Circle, a London association of architects, engineers, designers and planners who found refuge in England during this period.

Political complexion [wrote the editors of *The Architects' Journal* at the beginning of 1934] has only been openly identified with architectural forms recently. The post-war disease of aggressive nationalism is beginning to impose limitations upon architecture. The most brutal example is the censorship of design exercised by the sadistic boy scouts who are at present in charge of Germany's destiny. Germans have never been conspicuous for humour, and there is something dully academic as well as rawly juvenile about the deliberate suppression of what is known as "The Art of the Left" . . . what, we may ask, are the ideas of, shall we call him the Leader, about architecture that will represent the glory and the power, the empire, the earnestness, the wealth, the industry and the innate decency and sportmanship of England? Will the Leader favour banker's Classic or builder's Tudor?[47]

On the contrary, replied the British Union of Fascists' spokesmen, they wanted a new architecture but this would only come by using modern materials and techniques for a modern purpose. The failure of contemporary architecture was that it reflected individual licence instead of communal purpose. The cultural regeneration which Fascism was bringing to Europe would manifest itself in new virile styles of art.[48]

Such conventionally reasoned arguments were irrelevant when set against the overwhelming symbol of Hitler. To many intellectuals at first, the USSR had been a utopia that was admired from afar. While it could be agreed that Communism was the inevitable next phase of social democracy, few thought it desirable to insist upon its immediate implementation at home. It was just something to look forward to. The advent of Hitler changed all this. At once the issues became a matter of embattled opposites, of progress and retrogression, of right and wrong, of life and death. In this necessary simplification, the failings of Communism were overlooked or explained away while any Nazi achievements were simply denied. This attitude towards Communism culminated and died in the Spanish Civil War to be briefly reborn when the USSR became a British ally during the Second World War, and the spectre of Fascism was exorcised. For the intellectuals of the nineteen thirties this ideological confrontation was an inextricable part of life.

4 PRACTICE AND THEORY: AESTHETICS

In 1933 the firm of Tecton began their succession of outstanding buildings. Lubetkin, born in Russia in 1901, was sixteen years old at the time
of the revolution and took part in the artistic ferment that followed.
Leaving the Soviet Union in 1922, he travelled through Europe to Paris
where he completed his studies. With Jean Ginsberg he designed the
apartment building at 25 Avenue de Versailles which was illustrated in
The Architectural Review in 1932 when, dissatisfied with Beaux Arts
traditions, he went to England in search of a more conducive society.
Soon after his arrival, a chance meeting with Godfrey Samuel introduced
him to the AA graduating students who made up the Tecton partnership:
Lindsey Drake and R. T. F. Skinner were in their early twenties;
Anthony Chitty, Michael Dugdale, Valentine Harding and Samuel, who
had all previously been to either Oxford or Cambridge universities, were
slightly older. They were impressed by Lubetkin's talent and sense of
purpose for not only did he take to London advanced Continental
aesthetics but also a ruthless theorizing that paralleled and surpassed the
English involvement with sociology.

> [Soviet architects, he wrote] feel no animosity towards theories (as
> do their colleagues in capitalistic countries) because their ambition is
> not simply to build architecturally, but to build socialistically as well.[49]

The first commission for Tecton came from the London Zoo through the
friendship of Samuel and Lubetkin with a research anatomist, Solly
Zuckerman. The zoo having acquired two young gorillas, Tecton was
asked to house them. Then followed a series of buildings for animals the
most notable being the Penguin Pool of 1934 which, though diminutive,
gained an international reputation as the quintessential statement of the
new architectural aesthetic. Unconstrained by orthodox considerations
of functional planning and structural shelter, or by the users' tastes, the
architects constructed their imagery from the visual repertory of the

44

modern style. The famous intersecting ramps set over the pond captured the interpenetration of movement in the hovering of their taut concrete ribbons, depicting both the aims and methods of the style. Through slotted curving concrete walls, the spectators looked down on penguins seemingly enjoying spatial delights that the spectators were yet to experience. These animal environments were a prelude to the first large-scale modern human habitat in England, Highpoint One at Highgate, London, designed in 1933 and completed in 1935.

> For a long time [wrote Le Corbusier] I have dreamed of executing dwellings in such conditions for the good of humanity. The building at Highgate is an achievement of the first rank, and a milestone which will be useful to everybody.[50]

Le Corbusier's enthusiastic comments were based less on the architecture of Highpoint One than on its embryonic illustration of his theory of the vertical garden city. This upper-middle income group apartment house set at the front of a large garden on top of high ground was seen as a demonstration of the advantages of highrise living where the ground is left as a public park, contrasting with its horizontal neighbours that sprawl congestedly away from its pillared feet. Not only did the building follow Le Corbusier's general precepts but also ordered itself on his specific design program. Planned in the shape of a Cross of Lorraine, the main block is for the most part raised off the ground to let the freely shaped public rooms meander from the street in front, back and down to the garden at the rear. The roof is also formally independent of the rigid apartment structure. But while Highpoint One appears to follow its Continental model, its constructional method is far more sophisticated than that of Le Corbusier.

In this Tecton was helped by the engineer Ove Arup. British born of Scandinavian parents, Arup had studied in Copenhagen and Hamburg, where he had first worked with a Danish engineering construction firm before joining their London office in 1923. Influenced by meeting Lubetkin and wishing to involve himself with modern architectural design in reinforced concrete, from 1934 to 1938 he associated with another Danish contracting firm, J. L. Kier which, through an arrangement between Lubetkin and Arup, became responsible for the construction of Tecton's designs. Arup's belief that good architecture necessarily utilizes good construction was justified in Highpoint One where instead of superimposing a non loadbearing wall pattern against a structural grid, the reinforced concrete walls themselves are used as combined columns and beams. Form and structure are indivisible, a marrying of art and science that modern architects always preached but seldom practised. As Tecton moved from a functionalist to a formalist approach and Lubetkin became more concerned with getting effects built than with their constructive logic, Arup's contribution to the association became less decisive, but in initially showing that the modern aesthetic need not be just another applied style but could be a rational outcome of modern methods and materials, he established a standard against which to judge his contemporaries.

While the general appearance of Highpoint One suggests a close affinity to the work of Le Corbusier, the development of the main part of the building is fundamentally different. The apartment and vertical circulation enclosures used as structural solids virtually free the interior from any preconditioned arrangement, yet given these uncluttered volumes, there is no attempt at spatial exploitation. In place of architectural expression, a rigorous dimensional logic is used to organize the two and three bedroom apartment plans and eradicate all inefficient floor area from the compartmented unit. Kitchen, bath and circulation areas are immaculately squared off, the substantial living space being left to take its form from the surrounding rectangular rooms. This basic functional geometry is carried through the outside walls to set up the pattern of fenestration. There, against the window perforations, only the cyma balcony fronts introduce a dubious element into the composition. For the achievement of a rationalistic design is that everything appears to derive from the needs of the building itself without the obtrusion of the architect's personality.

The problem for the rationalist is one of neutrality, to find the midpoint between inadequacy and excess. The architect must impose his will upon the design up to the point where the solution appears to have an objective validity. Tecton's quasi-scientific approach was popularized through a series of explanatory diagrams initially prepared for visiting students and subsequently published in the architectural press showing the firm's method of analysis. To determine the overall form of the building, the financial need for sixty apartments was coordinated with the architectural requirements of aspect, prospect, privacy and ventilation, to give the parameters of a possible solution. Within these circumscribed boundaries, various forms were tested and the most fitting one selected. The attractiveness of this analytical method lay in its ostensible disregard of aesthetic considerations and its adherence to the point of view that anything that worked economically and well was automatically visually pleasing. Its manifest improbability was obscured by its apparent logic and the evident success of its use.

By 1936, however, when the older English members of the partnership had withdrawn from Lubetkin and the final version of Highpoint Two was being designed for the adjoining site, Tecton's rationalism was substantially modified. While Highpoint Two was built as a horizontal slab three duplexes high and four long with ground floor stilts and roof penthouse, the original intention was to use the same form as Highpoint One. The final building was the last of a series of six designs (the first four being submitted in the name of Robert Townsend)* and reached its end form ostensibly through a typically Tecton analytical process. The aesthetic development of this form, however, was treated as a separate study having its own surface discipline.

Standing in the garden [Anthony Cox commented on the finished building in *Focus*, a new magazine produced by AA students] and looking up at the two blocks, 1935 and 1938, it is clear that something has changed, and that the change is not due merely to the higher level of building, or to the use of a smooth, clean tile facing to the concrete. Highpoint I stands on tip-toe and spreads its wings; Highpoint II sits back on its haunches like Buddha. That this effect is deliberate, Tecton themselves would probably be the first to admit; one has the feeling that a *form* has been imposed on the rooms (which is an altogether different thing from giving the *rooms* form). It is as if, during the three years that separate the buildings, rigid conclusions have been reached as to what is formally necessary in architecture . . . The important point isn't whether or not one personally likes these formal conclusions, but whether one thinks that any such rigid conclusions are expedient . . . The intellectual approach which has produced what we know as modern architecture is fundamentally a functionalist approach. I take it that most of us do not need to argue about that. Functionalism is a rotten name for the antithesis of formalism, because it carries with it dehumanised ideas which nobody wishes to defend . . . but interpreted in a wide sense, I think the word conveys the method of work underlying this

*Lubetkin had little respect for conventional values and a predilection for intrigue that lasted through the sixteen years of Tecton's existence. For example during a slack period at the beginning of the partnership, he partnered A. V. Pilichowski in the design of a group of houses at Plumstead, London. This type of behaviour was foreign to his English colleagues. The Townsend plans that apparently were part of Tecton's overall submission for Highpoint Two were poorly arranged and one of the proposed designs had pseudo-historical detailing that could have been used either to conciliate or provoke the borough council. After the war, the reformed partnership broke up with recriminations and Lubetkin disowning his junior partner Lasdun.

movement . . . My contention is that the recent work of Tecton shows a deviation from this approach. It is more than a deviation of appearance; it implies a deviation of aim. It is more than an adjustment within legitimate limits; it is prepared to set certain formal values above use-values, and marks the re-emergence of the *idea* as the motive force. "Legitimate limits" is, of course, begging the question . . . nevertheless, I believe we can recognise certain limits as a sort of working hypothesis, and that there is a difference, blurred in the case of some architects and clear in the case of Tecton, between those who respect these limits and those who do not. These limits are not formal rules . . . they are limits of intention, by which certain aspects of the vast concept "building" are emphasised; they are deliberately selected as being those aspects which, in relation to the long-term development of modern architecture in an industrial economy, it is necessary to concentrate upon more than, though not necessarily to the exclusion of, other aspects.[51]

The horizontality of Highpoint Two is broken by the projection on both faces of the middle portion of the block, apparently expressing the difference in quality between the two large central apartments and the only slightly less luxurious apartments in the wings.* This differentiation on the garden side is carried out with some plausibility and elegance, contrasting the lightly framed glass and dark panel area with the perforated solidity of the sides. On the street elevation, however, the composition is completely unrelated to the sense of the interior. The slab is cut by two staircase boxes that hang down from an arbitrary roof projection sitting over balconies that run along the service side of the two central apartments. The wings remain as bland as Highpoint One except for the surface separation of finishes; the centre is a riot of glass brick, concrete, brick and glass. Epitomizing the new visual approach, the cantilevered free-shaped entrance canopy rests on the heads of Erechtheion caryatids. In their analytical way, the architects argued that no other solution was feasible: architectural supports conflicted with the scale of the building, contemporary sculpture was too personal for such a use: but such arguments are tenuous when twenty-five centuries divide an image and its use. No caryatids were considered necessary for the canopy of Highpoint One and if the canopy design of Highpoint Two made its support insoluble, the architects only had to alter its design. "Aestheticism", Lubetkin had written six years earlier, "the admiration

---

*The actual difference in quality is reflected in the rents which are from 5 to 10 percent higher in the centre apartments.

of aesthetically beautiful things, is characteristic of the *bourgeois* aesthetic".[52] Highpoint Two represents a design solution that transgresses the acceptable limits of rational architecture: its sensuousness attracts but its logic repels. *The Architectural Review* thought otherwise.

> The architectural character of the first Highpoint was essentially diagrammatic ... In the new block ... the conscious accentuation of certain forms and the variety of the materials used give a more human character to a facade that reads as a more deliberate architectural composition ... The difference, it may be emphasized, does not represent a divergence from strictly modern principles of design, but represents rather a development of modern design away from its early purist phase towards a maturer and more imaginative architectural language ... in its careful attention to the dignity that richness of modelling and texture can produce and its interest in a less abstract language it is an important move forward from functionalism.[53]

The Penguin Pool and Highpoint One were architectural symbols of international significance. The Tecton buildings that followed in the second half of the nineteen-thirties maintained their personality but lacked a unifying philosophy. The same keen rationalism that analysed everything in Highpoint One down to the hardware continued to be employed on the functional aspects of architectural problems but was also extended to regulate the problem of aesthetics itself. Whereas in Highpoint One the appearance of separate practical solutions of detail were related to an overall style with its own set of rules, in Highpoint Two the various parts each have a distinctive design expression. In a building such as the Finsbury Health Centre, London, designed in 1936 and completed in 1938, the shaped lecture hall is concrete, the duct-concealing curtain walls of the wings are teak and glass, the entrance hall is faced with glass bricks: each element is a reasonable solution but does not seem to be the only possible solution. This fragmentation of design caused by the lack of an overall stylistic discipline is covered by an applied composition that is in no way generated by the building itself but is used to provide an architectural surface.

Separating taste and common sense, Tecton returned to pre-modern values and became an enigma to its contemporaries. Underlying the mannered facades of its buildings is a forceful geometry derived from spaces logically disposed with clarity and economy. The Health Centre dominates its squalid surroundings by articulating itself on its site so as to establish its own axial grandeur; Highpoint Two makes its bulk felt by

E

the deep modelling of its main elevation. Their solidity has a unity of composition and rhythmical elaboration that organizes their distinctive version of the language of modern architecture into a powerful declaration of building art. And although their formalism provokes dissension, their functionalism commands respect by its unique intelligence.

While *The Architectural Review* approved of Highpoint Two, it was one of its editors, J. M. Richards, who popularized the opposing philosophy. Richards, an AA graduate in his twenties, had worked abroad for a few years before joining the Architectural Press in 1933 as assistant editor of *The Architects' Journal*. By 1935 when he changed to *The Architectural Review*, he had superseded Shand as the theorist of the modern movement.

There is an essential difference, Richards argued, between the products of the handicraft age of the past and the present industrial system. "The difference is, in brief, that which lies between a humanistic aesthetic and an abstract one. . . Design, as with culture, is becoming abstract rather than humanistic."[54] We live in a scientific world and architecture is an expression of it. As with science, we are no longer satisfied with unexplained oddities but search for the general rule; the individual work of art is replaced by mass produced design.

> The bane of the nineteenth century [Richards wrote in an article on 'The condition of architecture and the principle of anonymity'] was the celebrity-architect: the Renaissance idea of the individual glorified over the Renaissance sense of artistic unity. And architecture cannot afford to be an affair of the individual. It is only when the individual innovation becomes assimilated into a regional tradition that it can be regarded as culturally valid.[55]

Like Le Corbusier in his Purist phase, Richards thought that the designer's function was to find typical forms to serve typical people, but whereas Le Corbusier divided his types into the "mass of people" and the "intellectuals" and proposed a somewhat different treatment for the two, Richards wanted to be an equal part of the society that he served. He saw "the aesthetic virtue of regimentation" and cited Lewis Mumford on the parade ground as

> the prototype of modern industrial organization with its tendency to turn the individual into an impersonal unit, personal determination on part of which is a hindrance to efficient action instead of an aid to it. Indeed many characteristics of the modern aesthetic existed separately in various phases of the dehumanization and mechanization of labour in Egypt . . .[56]

He might have cited the Nuremberg rallies, but unlike those who believed in a controlling elite who were superhumanly above the masses, Richards' thesis implied a universal equality with himself as the highest common denominator. So long as art remained personal there was no proof that it had any cultural validity; only when it was taken up by society could it be recognized as truly being art. Acceptance by the common man was needed to enable architecture "to make the transition from its adolescent stage as the conscious cult of an intelligentsia to its maturer stage as the unconscious expression of a culture."[57] Richards saw society as a homogeneous whole, once again brought together by a contemporary cosmology. As the acceptable style for this society had obviously been influenced through individual acts of creation by European and American architects, it was necessary to formulate a simple linear system of architectural history. That is, a social environment comes into being, it is experienced and portrayed by men of insight who are more sensitive than their contemporaries, and then as it becomes more familiar through both its existence and its artistic manifestations, it is absorbed into the bloodstream of everyday activity. In modern architectural terms, the industrial revolution had changed the lives of the masses which could no longer be represented by stylistic revivals, Gropius and his associates had created an expression of society as it really was, now the ordinary people could inhabit a world of form that corresponded to life as they experienced it. Unfortunately, this simplified theory failed to observe that society is constantly changing, that the nature of change lies in the push and pull of individuals in large and small numbers, and that to express society is rather more difficult than to express oneself.

Richards' general argument is based on the history of architecture as self-contained styles with Modern following Renaissance, but whereas the common view was to see the previous epoch as a biological process of birth, fulfilment and decadence, Richards observed that the style progressed from isolated men of genius, such as Brunelleschi and Michelangelo, to the universal level of Georgian good taste. He overlooked the fact that while 350 years elapsed between the Pazzi Chapel and the Royal Crescent at Bath, only forty years separated the major work of Louis Sullivan from England in the nineteen-thirties. If the pace of change had increased to this extent, it was unlikely that a modern building style could be long consolidated before it became obsolete. The spirit of inventiveness, which Richards noted as a characteristic of the contemporary involvement with science, encouraged the architect to emulate the engineer. While science is additive and comprehensive, art may be considered finite and fragmentary. The architect wavered between a traditional immutability, suitably limited to a cultural epoch, and the ambition to be a spokesman of the twentieth century. The 1921 Delage, commented a reviewer of *Towards a New Architecture* in 1927, compares as unfavourably with a Sunbeam of today as a 1907 Humber compares with the Delage.[58]

It is clear that the architect's freedom to explore his own eccentricities is largely delineated by society. His practice of his art is circumscribed by his client's taste and the inherent conservatism of both building codes and industry. Yet opportunities within these limitations are evidenced by the very pioneers who first are thought to respond to the new conditions of society. If Le Corbusier could succeed in academic Paris and Frank Lloyd Wright in the philistine mid-western United States, then a similar achievement is possible for an individual in a culturally more enlightened society. So long as the creation of a style is not restricted by centralized control, it will always change by interaction within society. It is most unlikely that a political democracy of many millions can develop such a unified taste as to permit a continuing single expression of it.

Of course, Richards did not mean that architecture ought to express the people of a society, only its spirit. And even this must be worthy of expression.

> The Victorian age [he wrote] comes in for a lot of abuse, much of it quite justifiable; but the result is a common belief that architects at this time were in some way incapable of producing anything but what was ugly. The best architects of the nineteenth century were, as a matter of fact, men of remarkable ability and enthusiasm who in other circumstances would have been producing fine architecture. They had all the talent necessary. It was the times that had gone wrong.[59]

Similarly Richards condemned the German neo-Classical buildings which so rightly seemed to echo the majority Nazi party, and the English neo-Classical buildings commissioned by the electorate of the over-whelmingly conservative representative English parliament. It appeared that architecture as an abstract art was to express the abstracted significance of the society. Stripped of its human excrescences, life was potentially as systematic as science. The surface may be torn by strikes, assassinations and approaching war, but underneath was an inviolable pattern of order typified by the imperturbable machine. This was to be the obverse of the coin. On the one side the machine turning man into a goose-stepping steel-clad moron with debased sensibilities; on the other, man reaping the benefit of the machine's bounty and emulating its inherent dignity.

> The machine, [wrote Richards] instead of being an extension of his own faculties becomes, for man, a mechanical equivalent of nature: a physical manifestation of the world of order and scientific thinking, giving him a sense, in inventing power machinery, of himself contributing to the orderliness of the universe.[60]

This view of modern architecture as an expression of the industrialization of society is a literal application of a simplified version of the cultural theory of Marx and had potent overtones in the nineteen thirties. Equally important, Richards' advice for the practising architect was easy to follow: as a "negative rather than a competitive environment is essential" to counteract the "growing complication of modern existence" so buildings should be simple and repetitive.[61] This appeal to anonymity suited the abilities of the British group of architects; belief in a fixed style spared them further questioning.

Except for Tecton, there was general conformity to the basic rules of modern architecture. Within this stylistic limitation only Connell, Ward and Lucas produced a consistent series of buildings. Their practice consisted almost entirely of houses, the design of which had much in common with that of the Dutch followers of de Stijl. Wall, roof and window elements are used as opaque and transparent planes delineating cubic volumes but whereas the typical building of the modern style maintains a simple volumetric skin, suggestive of the machine in its clarity of form and surface, the work of Connell, Ward and Lucas has an insistent harshness that accentuates the blocking out process of creating the design. There is nothing reposeful about their buildings. The rectangular parts of the buildings are stacked against and on top of each other developing an angular rhythm that remains undiluted even by the occasional curve. Each possible idiosyncrasy of plan or section is exploited to enrich the composition so that the total effect has a crude vitality that was disliked by their more temperate contemporaries. This differentiation between the work of the partnership and their colleagues was underlined by Henry-Russell Hitchcock when in selecting English modern architecture for exhibition at the Museum of Modern Art, New York, in 1937, he represented the partnership by two early works of Lucas. The quality of the work of Connell, Ward and Lucas, he wrote in the catalogue, could be judged by their detailing which showed that "the central principles of design are not altogether clear or sufficiently coherent".* Yet the clumsiness (or vigour) of their copings, sills, sash and rails is certainly in accord with the character of the whole; as is their planning. The rooms are smaller or larger boxes opened up with glass slots and walls, conveniently located with simple access halls. Elegance is replaced by straightforward simplicity. It is the limitation of their work that it never attained a serene finality, never found an absolute image that would summarize their achievement. But few such buildings were built in Britain and these were not part of any progressive development. The modulated glass facade of the Peter Jones store was designed by architects of no further consequence; Fry's Sun House, at Hampstead in London, with its eloquent balconies and canopies exquisitely balanced against an immaculately fenestrated facade, came between his slow struggle against a neo-Georgian training and his occupation with an indifferent modernism.

It is almost impossible to name any one man as the leader in modern architecture in England to-day, [wrote F. R. S. Yorke and Colin Penn in 1939] but it is perhaps Maxwell Fry who should be given first place by his colleagues. He has been responsible for a number of houses in which rational planning and delicacy of treatment are combined with a precise selection of materials to produce a fine finish.[62]

Between 1927 and 1935, Fry was the building design partner in the firm of Adams, Thompson and Fry which was mainly involved in large scale planning schemes. Its prize entry for the Birmingham Civic Centre competition in 1927 was neo-Classical. His design for the Kemsley Village Club House in Kent, built in 1929, was neo-Georgian; for the house Ridge End in Wentworth, Surrey, built in 1930, it was cottage vernacular. His RIBA building competition submission of 1932 used a conventional updating of traditional effects. His first building completed in the modern architectural manner was Sassoon House in Camberwell, London, a low rental apartment block constructed during 1934.

Fry was almost unique in his acceptance by the various shades of architectural opinion. Together with Emberton he was both a member

---

*Henry-Russell Hitchcock, "Modern architecture in England", *Modern Architecture in England*, edited by the Museum of Modern Art, New York 1937, p. 38. Hitchcock visited England in the summer of 1936. He contrasted the detailing of Connell, Ward and Lucas with that of Tecton whose "details are always interesting . . . because they flow logically from some central principle of design".

of the MARS group and the RIBA council* but whereas Emberton's influence declined during the critical years of the mid nineteen thirties, Fry's reached its climax.

His work during the few years following his adoption of the modern architectural style has an aesthetic maturity that was rare. The plans of such buildings as the Kensal House apartments in London and the house at Kingston, Surrey, are neat; their structure is sensible: neither factor is of exceptional interest. It is their composition that gives Fry's buildings such authority. With perfect taste, solids and voids are disposed as a surface background to a sculptural play of rhapsodic elements. Shadowed in sunlight, his buildings are beautiful to look at.

The majority in Britain either would not, or could not, impose an architectural personality on their designs and their buildings were generally both muddled and nondescript. A typical house such as that by Yorke at Iver, Buckinghamshire, completed in 1936, has a small complicated plan whose projections appear to derive more from bad planning than design as the resultant inner spaces are neither practical nor interesting and the outer form is too disjointed for its size. Its distinction is in the fact of its existence. Compared to the buildings of the previous decade produced by the masters in Germany and France, those in Britain were predominantly mediocre. They lack the necessary ruthlessness that lets a work of art find its own fulfilment. The architect, restricted by non-artistic considerations but wishing to produce a building of artistic import, assimilates the prerequisites of his design so that by the time he consciously starts to work, he is as free in his creativity as a painter or a sculptor. When practical considerations impinge upon a building after its germination is complete, it falters between art and design. The reason for a certain projection or opening cannot only be its function but must at the same time have imagistic significance. Pleasing proportions or fashionable motifs cannot hide a basically non-artistic conception. The group in Britain avoided questions of art. Modern architecture is beautiful, wrote Yorke, because "modern materials and construction and the shapes produced by them have an intrinsic beauty".[63] Their aim was to emulate the machine engineer who finds virtue in necessity.

This functionalistic approach, however, was largely spurious. Unlike the machine engineer who treats his predecessor as a springboard for improvement, they were content to take over the diagnoses and remedies of their Continental predecessors without regard to differences in time and place. Their secondhand questions had preconceived answers so that

*Fry was an associate member of the RIBA council 1933–7; Emberton, 1933–8.

the smooth glazed flat roofed reinforced concrete structures that were fashionably obligatory indiscriminately found their way into country, suburb and city where they were used as a cure-all for rich and poor. The results were disquieting. In the wet, dirty, atmosphere of London, even Highpoint One with its close collaboration between designer and constructor found its columns spalling from the rust of its reinforcement. Sassoon House, claimed as representing a major advance in the design of low rental dwellings, has ungalvanized steel windows in poorly detailed openings that contributed to its early deterioration. The buildings generally had initial constructional failures, were expensive to maintain, and difficult to alter. While the hazards of pioneering and lack of money were the reasons often used in excuse, the contrasting durability between the traditional and modern shows that logic was often abandoned when it conflicted with dogma.* The group found constructional assistance in the quantity surveyor, Cyril Sweett, but as the decade progressed it learned little from experience. This anti-scientific neglect of methodical building research was not offset by any refinement of style. The Continental masters sacrificed function to art while insisting that art derives from function. Their followers in England sacrificed function too, but, beguiled by the myth, also rejected a direct involvement with style.

The work of the German immigrants had little effect on the British group except to raise its morale and give it international prestige.† On his arrival in England in 1933, Mendelsohn had joined Chermayeff in partnership and together they entered and won the competition for the

---

*Arup later recalled: "Whilst I was a member of the executive committee of MARS, we spent a whole year discussing what modern architecture really meant, and what MARS really stood for. It was supposed to mean 'Modern Architectural Research Group', but what kind of research? Apparently, it was supposed to be into heat and sound insulation of walls, acoustics, light angles and so on. I pointed out that this was engineering or building research and that we, as a group predominantly of architects, were neither competent or equipped to undertake it. We should do architectural research: planning research. Lubetkin maintained that no two architects would be able to agree on architectural questions—that was Art, a personal matter—and that architectural research was nonsense." See Ove Arup, "Art and architecture. The architect: engineer relationship", RIBAJ, LXXIII, 1966, p. 354. For insight into the factors involved in marketing a new material such as reinforced concrete which was theoretically cheap but expensive in small-scale use, see Marian Bowley, *The British Building Industry: Four studies in response and resistance*, Cambridge 1966, also Marian Bowley, *Innovations in Building Materials: An economic study*, London 1960.

†The partnerships of Mendelsohn and Chermayeff, and Gropius and Fry, were dramatically represented in Chelsea, London, where they designed adjacent houses completed in 1936.

Bexhill Pavilion in Sussex. Adjudicated by Tait, the planning of the building, completed in 1935, is imposing in its simplicity; the forms have vitality and grace. The spaces, however, are peculiarly solid and even though the rooms are largely glazed, their geometry and detail of structure and opening separate them from each other and the vistas outside. Similarly, visual penetration from outside in is prevented by overhangs and the accentuation of trim. This gravity of effect was foreign to the taste of the younger British architects. Modern architecture was light, open, pleasant; Mendelsohn's work was too ponderous.

His use of structure was more to their liking. The engineering consultant for Bexhill Pavilion was Felix Samuely,[64] an Austrian immigrant whom Mendelsohn had met in Berlin. In 1933, after a few years in the USSR, he had found himself without a suitable country of residence and had decided to settle in Britain. He received his first job from Arup for whom he did the detailed calculations of the Penguin Pool structure. For the Bexhill Pavilion he designed the first completely welded steel structure in Britain. Unlike Arup whose services while he remained with J. L. Kier were linked with those of his company, Samuely as a consulting engineer was widely used by the architects of the modern movement including Emberton, Coates, and Connell, Ward and Lucas. His structural mastery gave modern architects the benefits of modern techniques without basically modifying their forms. The Bexhill Pavilion looks like a reinforced concrete building; in fact, its reinforced concrete walls are hung from steel trusses between the main columns, while the elegant north staircase is also suspended from two hidden cantilevering steel roof beams. Samuely permitted modern buildings to be more refined than if serviced by a conventional consultant but his virtuosity was usually hidden by the architecture. The Simpson's building, London, designed by Emberton, is an example. Having made clever use of a storey high Vierendeel truss above the ground floor, it was disallowed by the London County Council just before it was erected, yet while an ordinary girder system had to be hurriedly installed, the facade design remained unaltered. Since the battle of the styles of the previous century, the argument had raged as to whether the expression of structure was a necessary quality of superior architecture. The Gothic school compared the honesty of Salisbury with the falsity of St. Paul's; the Classic school compared the refinement of St. Paul's with the crudity of Salisbury: modern architects combined a theoretical obsession with truth with an actual involvement with appearance.

Mendelsohn's work had been too personal for his Continental contemporaries; it was equally so for his adopted colleagues who looked back to the Bauhaus as their exemplar. In 1934 Gropius himself emigrated to Britain where the RIBA mounted an exhibition in his honour. A few years earlier Pritchard had bought some land for a house but had been persuaded by his architect, Coates, to build an apartment block as an investment instead. With its elementarist imagery of cantilevered galleries and raking escape stairways looking better in axonometric drawing than in reality, the newly completed Lawn Road Flats in Hampstead, London became a haven for many refugees.* Through Shand, Pritchard invited Gropius as a guest, offering him a free apartment and meals from the central kitchen. Although he failed to find him employment in other abortive land development projects, Pritchard set up the Isokon Furniture Company with Gropius as design controller and for them Marcel Breuer, brought to Britain in 1935 through Shand's further overtures, designed his internationally famous bent plywood long chair.

During this period Gropius associated unofficially with Fry, at first while he was still a partner of Adams and Thomson and later when he had set up his own practice. In 1936 they entered into formal partnership but their only commission of importance was completed after Gropius had left the country.

The invitation to design the Impington Village College near Cambridge, completed in 1939, resulted from a meeting through Pritchard with Henry Morris, the Cambridgeshire Education Secretary. As a cultural centre for a cluster of villages, it augments daytime children's classes with evening adult education and community activities. The building has little imagistic interest except for its centrifugal plan. The interior spaces are commonplace and their connecting circulation links fail at those points where larger and smaller volumes meet. The exterior form, potentially interesting with its extended massing, is broken up by the variation of its treatment which ranges from the use of glass walls in the classroom wing to the large windows cut into the structural brick side walls of the fan-shaped assembly hall. Yet the college is pleasing in its simple materials and scale. With its fine pastoral setting, its unpretentious brickwork and the meandering ease of its disposition, it stands apart from its doctrinaire contemporaries.

That the British work of Gropius was without influence can be seen

---

*John Summerson cites the Lawn Road Flats as the most memorable British building of the nineteen-thirties. (See his introduction to Trevor Dannatt, *Modern Architecture in Britain*, London 1959). In 1946 after inevitable wartime neglect, Cyril Connolly's *Horizon* magazine awarded its entrant the second prize of £10 in a competition for ugly buildings. (See XIV, 1946, p. 343).

in the results of the school building competition organized by the
News Chronicle, a London newspaper, in 1936 and won by Denis Clarke
Hall, a young AA graduate.[65] His design has similar components to the
contemporaneous Impington Village College but is substantially lighter
in form, space and structure. The prize winners of the two hundred and
fifty entries submitted to show how schools could be improved were
either of the orthodox modern movement or closely related in their
progressiveness. For by the second half of the nineteen-thirties Hitchcock could write that "it is not altogether an exaggeration to say that
England leads the world in modern architectural activity".[66] The new
style had replaced commonsense eclecticism as the *au courant* standard
before Gropius had built anything in Britain.

By that time the students of schools of architecture such as those at
Leeds and Liverpool were producing modern architectural projects.[67]
The change over at the AA was more dramatic. On Robertson's resignation the direction of the school was divided between H. S. Goodhart-
Rendel and E. A. A. Rowse. Rowse began to liberalize the design
policy but Goodhart-Rendel, occupying the senior position, soon exerted
pressure to return the school to Beaux Arts practices. Caught in the
middle with opinions of their own, the students threatened to go on
strike but in the ensuing conflict first Rowse and then Goodhart-Rendel
withdrew from the school. The historical position of Goodhart-Rendel
who had been president of the RIBA and Slade Professor of Fine Art at
Oxford University was summed up in an appreciation published in the
AA *Journal*.

His time at the AA has coincided with a period of mental excitement
among the students. The AA, like most of the architectural schools
throughout the country has reacted vigorously to political-social-
architectural doctrines which are generally spoken of as "left-wing".
Under the stimulus of these ideas much excellent, even brilliant,
work has been produced, and never in the school's history has a
greater keenness existed both among masters and students. To a man
such as Goodhart-Rendel, equipped with a highly critical mind, a
keen sense of continuity, and an unusual breadth of culture, this
fervent but narrow ideology must have presented problems of no
ordinary complexity. A lesser man would have swum with the
stream and enjoyed hero-worship, or else tried to impose his own
ideals. Mr. Goodhart-Rendel had too much sympathy with the
young to do the latter, too much conviction to do the former.[68]

The avant-garde had won its place. To celebrate its maturity, the MARS group mounted a large exhibition in the New Burlington Galleries in London at the beginning of 1938. Entitled 'New Architecture', but ordered on the classical definition of 'commoditie, firmenes and delight', its various sections showed building needs and contemporary techniques, and how modern architecture had synthesized the two. Actual rooms were set up as examples and a large number of photographs and models illustrated the extent of modern architectural practice. The group was proud of its achievements.

> Today, [the catalogue stated] a singular degree of unanimity has been reached among architects whose outlook is independent of academic tradition and prejudice. We seem to have attained one of those periodic *plateaux* which occur in the historical ascent of every intellectual movement, and which facilitate the permeation of newly formed concepts into the main body of professional and public opinion.[69]

Seven thousand people visited the exhibition and if *The Times* review[70] reflected informed conservatism, then modern architecture had indeed become respectable if not welcome.

The peak, however, had already been passed. The previous year Gropius, who had not been offered the directorship, then vacant, of the Cambridge University school of architecture, accepted an appointment to Harvard University and was soon followed by Breuer. Mendelsohn virtually withdrew from Britain and his practice was mainly continued in Palestine. The partnership of Connell, Ward and Lucas dissolved in 1939 through lack of work. And as the decade came to an end, there were more important issues than architectural style.

5 THEORY AND PRACTICE: SOCIOLOGY

The twentieth century architect looked back at the preceding century and saw that his profession had contributed little to the reforms that paralleled the evils of industrialization. While architects argued over the suitability of various styles for individual buildings, laymen from Robert Owen to Ebenezer Howard searched for an overall urban solution that could cope with the needs of an industrialized society. It was Le Corbusier's achievement, following from Tony Garnier, to extend the aesthetic principles of modern architecture into a potent visual image of the total city. A modern architecture could exist in a conventional environment—it had flowered with Wright in a Chicago suburb—but there remained a fundamental opposition between the building and its surroundings. While cities develop over centuries and architects only practice through a lifetime it seems inevitable that a compromise is the most that can be achieved but for Le Corbusier this was unacceptable. Using Baron Haussmann as an embryonic precedent he demanded the demolishing of existing cities and their rebuilding in a logical manner. His aim was not to build new communities but to recondition the old. Aware that cities had historical reasons for being where they were and could not be arbitrarily moved, he was convinced that obsolete cities should be replaced in their entirety. With his central skyscrapers surrounded by serpentine blocks set in parkland through which fast moving traffic competed with soaring aeroplanes above, an image equal to the perforated box was given to the modern architectural city. The microcosmic *machine à habiter* was provided a setting in the macrocosmic *ville radieuse. The City of Tomorrow*, translated from his book Urbanisme[71] by Etchells and published in Britain in 1929, was received by its reviewers with extremes of condemnation and eulogy. "M. Le Corbusier's city", wrote A. Trystan Edwards in *The Architectural Review*, "is a dead city and it represents nothing more or less than architectural nihilism."[72] "It is not a dream or

61

but human's are very emotion creatures

a fantasy", commented *The Studio*, "but a sober solution of practical problems arrived at by a process of clear and precise thinking."[73]

By the end of the nineteen-twenties, after the decline of the post-First World War boom and the confrontation of the General Strike, many people looked to planning as a panacea. The Labour party was committed to the central control of industry through various means including its nationalization. The Liberal party under Lloyd George's direction also urged the placing of major industries under public boards. Even enlightened Conservatives rejected the doctrine of uncontrolled free enterprise. This general belief in the need for governmental planning was evidenced in the Town and Country Planning Act in 1932.

> I should not venture, particularly on this occasion, [stated the Conservative Minister of Health, Sir Hilton Young, during the Depression] to propose a Measure to the House even with the most harmless intentions, if it were not appropriate to the general state of the country at the present time, and it is because I think this Bill is particularly appropriate, in view of the great national need for economy, that I have so little hesitation in commending it to the House today . . . Formerly, we might have been more or less haphazard in developing our national resources, but now I suggest, in order to get full value out of the resources of the country, we have to plan and look ahead in order to be able to fit everything in. I will ask the House to turn its mind back to the position of affairs that prevailed when the towns were growing up at the beginning of the last century, at the time of the dawn of the great industrial revolution. At that time, all things were done in haste, without foresight, and I am sure that nobody who looks at the older regions of the great industrial areas of this country can but feel it was a tragedy that that industrial civilisation should have been allowed to grow up haphazard and without thought, and nobody who sees the condition, as I say, of the older areas of these towns but must be fairly persuaded that it is our business to see that there shall be reasonable foresight exercised in their growth and in their development for the future.[74]

The semantic misappropriation of the term *to plan* by architects who failed to see the difference between the word used to denote the arrangement of spaces and its meaning as a scheme of action, encouraged them to promote themselves as social leaders. As early as the first town planning conference, held in Britain before the First World War, the profession had claimed that town planning was merely an extension of architectural design.[75] By the nineteen-thirties the belief had been extended to cover any form of planning and it was so widely held by architects that the RIBA president, Sir Giles Gilbert Scott, designer of Liverpool Cathedral, could write as a foreword to an exhibition catalogue of International Architecture held in 1934 that

the Institute has not arranged this Exhibition merely as an entertainment. It is avowedly an exhibition with a purpose. The purpose is to demonstrate the architect as a PLANNER, and as one of the most important servants of the community, with a valuable contribution to make towards an improvement in the art of living.[76]

To the modern architect, this interrelationship between architecture and society was of primary importance. A building was not a work of art but a social statement. Impington Village College was considered important as a prototype centre for a new rural life and was praised as such in the wartime Scott Report of the Committee on Land Utilisation in Rural Areas.[77] Lawn Road Flats was designed for up to date inhabitants who travelled lightly and wanted minimum space and maximum service, and reached its apogee with its use by refugees.

What is the essential intention of the art of architecture? [wrote Coates in *Unit One* the publication of a group of artists and architects (the other architect being Lucas) formed in 1933 to promote the modern style]. Reduced to its simplest elements, architecture is the art of providing *ordered shelter* for a multitude of human activities . . . Every change in human conditions brings with it new possibilities of relationships of human needs, and the necessity to order them anew, to give them form, and freedom, and fullness and richness of life. . . . As architects of the ultimate human and material scenes of the new order, we are not so much concerned with the formal elements of 'style' as with an *architectural* solution of the social and economic problems of today . . . As creative architects we are concerned with a Future which must be *planned*, rather than a Past which must be *patched up* . . .[78]

It was inconceivable to the modern architect that traditional architecture could solve the building problems of the new society. It had seemed natural for the Pioneer Health Centre to have been designed in concrete and glass. Where, as in Cambridgeshire, the Impington Village College was preceded by three other (though smaller) colleges built in a traditional manner, they were simply ignored.

While other social building problems were tackled as they arose, the focus of the modern architect's concern was working class housing.

"The modern town", wrote McGrath, "is judged not by its town-halls and public buildings but by its housing".[79] That more conventional architects had some sympathy with this range of involvement can be seen in their collaboration with the MARS group members Fry and McGrath, and the proponents of modernism, Towndrow and Duncan, on the committee for the International Architecture exhibition which almost coincided with the first MARS group exhibit.

Invited to contribute to a 'New Homes for Old Housing' exhibit at Olympia in London, the MARS group presented an investigation it had started as a research project the previous year into the working class London borough of Bethnal Green. Using propaganda methods of display, its panels analysed the characteristics of a slum. No solutions were given but they were promised for the future.

> The next steps will be an analysis of Needs and an analysis of Means whereby the chaotic conditions here set out can best be resolved into conditions of more civilized living; and, the sociological problems having been first tackled, the Group will be able to approach on a sound basis the problems within the boundaries more popularly supposed to limit the architect's function. The absence of any designs for buildings [added *The Architects' Journal*] is indeed the most notable and encouraging symptom of the right approach that characterizes this exhibition of architects' work.[80]

But while his thoughts may have been with the oppressed public, the modern architect's practice was bought by private patrons. Commissioned to design individual houses, he found justification in that the problems to be solved in the individual house are not greatly dissimilar to those facing the municipal architect. "In both cases it is the problem of economy of space, efficiency in function and provision of maximum opportunity for the well-being of the inhabitants."[81]

The modern house became the symbol of the new architecture, a sample of the world to be: in 1934 Yorke published *The Modern House*, McGrath *Twentieth Century Houses*.

The significance of the house was at two levels. To those who were committed to improving the material condition of society, it was a statement of a rationalist approach that could raise standards and cut costs.

> In so far as the modern architect is concerned [Yorke wrote in *The Modern House*] the villa has had, and will continue to have, a great importance as the cheapest building unit for examination and

experiment . . . since the architect can gain real experience of new construction only in actual building work, he is most likely to find in the villa the most easily accessible unit for research.[82]

To others primarily interested in the art of architecture, the house was a research image of the new aesthetic.

The future [ends McGrath in *Twentieth Century Houses*] is in the hollow of our hands. In the wide windows of the twentieth-century house are framed the white towns of to-morrow and the clear-cut buildings of men as awake as ever the Greeks were to the fullest pleasures of living. What other road is there to take but into these surprising distances?[83]

This difference in intent was not evident in the building's appearance but rested in the philosophy of its designer. Both Connell, Ward and Lucas, and Fry designed both private houses and working class flats, yet to the former each commission was sufficient within itself while to the latter the one was ostensibly an exercise for the other.* For as Fry wrote:

The small house, fulfilling still a deep want that certain happily placed sections of the community have money to gratify, provides the architect with the means of putting into practice ideas which have their final application in the service of the wider community—when the community is prepared to receive them.[84]

At the beginning of the modern movement in Britain, this difference in intent had little importance; those who formed the MARS group were united in their modernism. By the end of the year, however, political involvements had begun to make themselves felt.† As with social

---

*Those by Connell, Ward and Lucas are Kent House, St Pancras, London, completed in 1935. See above for those by Fry.

†Memories of these days are apt to be clouded by personalities and later events. Connell does "not recall that politics unduly flavoured the ideal of the MARS group. However intensely may have burned a political ideal in any individual breast, the humour infused by the occasional appearance on our screen of John Betjeman and Morton Shand leavened the group and brought into perspective many of the views held by this precious cell of intense and angry young men". Another ex-member, Hazen Sise, recollects that "although there were people in the group who might now describe themselves as right-wingers, my memory is that they were all fashionably left-of-centre in those days. When in 1934 . . . I was project manager for the group while we were doing our first exhibition on housing: a sociological and economic analysis of the borough of Bethnal Green, I had to read the riot act when I found that practically everyone was proposing

reformers of the nineteenth century, concern for the public welfare had no single motivation. The liberal argued that there was nothing essentially wrong with the capitalist system and that imperfections could be remedied by intelligent adjustments. The Socialist replied that the imperfections were inherent in the capitalist system and demanded a society where reform would not be necessary. The economic system in the nineteenth century, wrote the left wing theorist John Strachey in much the same words as William Morris had used a generation earlier, for all its many injustices had worked.[85] All that seemed to be required was a sustained process of reform to alleviate its worst characteristics. Contemporary events appeared to show that this evolutionary process had been reversed. The 1929 depression, the overwhelming parliamentary defeat of the Labour and Liberal parties in 1931, and the acquisition of power by Hitler in 1933, altered the balance of the choice. At the time of the General Strike in 1926, the students of the AA (including such liberals as the future RIBA librarian Edward Carter) could patriotically answer the call to help defeat the workers by acting as police and railwaymen. Ten years later AA students were registering their alarm at "the Fascist elements in this country attacking progressive art".[86] The speed at which the National Socialists had destroyed all democratic institutions in Germany frightened the liberal intellectual into abandoning the slow process of social reform for the direct political methods of Socialism. For the architect involved with the urban environment, the social implications of right and left wing politics were inherent in his conditions of practice. The extent to which this was understood by modern architects was set out by Chermayeff and Richards in an article in *The Architects' Journal* published at the beginning of 1935 and entitled 'A Hundred Years Ahead'.

Their diary of future events whimsically included such items as the discovery of an insulation board made from celery and the consequent revival of British agriculture, but intertwined with architectural flippancy was their interpretation of the relationship between architecture and politics.

It was between 1936–1965 during the first Socialist reconstruction

to abandon a Saturday afternoon work session in order to turn out and greet the hunger marchers".

On the other side, H. T. B. Griggs, whose wife was the British Union of Fascists' chief women's organizer, still writes of "the architecture of international socialism" as practised and advocated by those like Chermayeff, Lubetkin and Richards, while Aitken (see below) remembers that "there *were* a number of modern architects at the time who were mildly socialistic; 'Pink Intellectuals' was a current term I believe".

period, the authors wrote, that the government took over control of the building industry.

> Private builders and material makers, forced out of their rings of controlled prices and the competition which was the cause of waste and of the making of unnecessary things, made the discovery after the first shock that a new sort of producing-organization was possible which put an end to the waste and serious losses of the old system of competition. It became general for all important parts to be made in fixed designs and sizes, and greater use was made of this. Building became cheaper and quicker . . . The step from controlled building to a New Art was a short one. By a development of the sense of the beautiful which is in all of us, men came to take a pleasure not only in certain buildings but in all buildings, and with this came the desire for the same high quality in the art of painting, stonework and design generally.[87]

Against this Socialist rationalism which finally triumphed with airship towns housing ten thousand people each, the Fascists, in a governmental interlude leading to an inter-continental war, built structures "rooted in fear", starting with disused coal mines and then blasting holes and building underground.

The editors hoped that the article would be read in the spirit in which it was intended and invited readers' suggestions and opinions. While no one seemed interested in purely architectural clairvoyance, caring little if shuttering became obsolete in 1971 or not, the reaction to the political predictions was out of all proportion to its provocation.

> The tragedy of the Jew [wrote a young architect, Keith Aitken, to *The Architects' Journal*, apparently referring to Chermayeff] appears to be his unfailing ability to arouse antagonism wherever he goes. It is his own fault, if it be a fault to act in accordance with one's nature; but it is nevertheless unfortunate, for he wounds both himself and the nation which, in the end, has to throw him out . . . If we in England are to avoid this depressing prospect we must be on our guard against too readily drinking in Jewish-Communist doctrine, even when it is disguised in the most seductive of concrete and glass clothes.[88]

After publishing numerous letters, the editors of *The Architects' Journal* closed the correspondence, "pure politics as such not being within our province",[89] though not before Chermayeff and Richards had affirmed their "being on the side of socialism and internationalism while they appear to be the only means of achieving world peace".[90] In the same issue of the magazine, Skinner announced a new architects' organization.

We are obstructed and prevented from assuming our proper social responsibilities by reactionary economic and political forces . . . which are tending unmistakably in one direction. That direction, in our opinion, is towards Fascism and its concomitant, war. Already the brutality and the terror of the one have reduced the living standards of millions in Italy, Germany and Austria, while the preparations for the other become daily more plain. One of our first tasks . . . is to fight for higher working-class standards in housing and general conditions—the two cannot be separated—and we believe that architects holding these views could usefully organize themselves.[91]

The student section of this group, the Architects and Technicians Organization, was soon addressed by Chermayeff. In 'A Hundred Years Ahead', the authors had argued that without material comfort, ordinary people could not be expected to appreciate art, but that with the widespread benefits of Socialism it would become possible "for those who had had all power of feeling forced out of their minds and bodies by the unequal fight for existence and the impossibly low level of living to have an eye for art and an interest in ideas."[92] Chermayeff's lecture approached the problem from the other end. The only patrons who could encourage art at a public scale were the corporations and government. As both were in partnership to exploit the working-class majority of the population, the socially committed architect had to work for socialism where the government represented the people. In a capitalist society, the architect was merely a sycophant. "Architects can no longer concern themselves with construction in a separated professional compartment. They must participate in the reconstruction of society."[93] Unfortunately they were limited to small private commissions.

Confronted by the same situation, and prompted by the exigencies of practice, Connell, with the concurrence of Ward and Lucas, decided to outwit the establishment. His scheme was to enter competitions, win them by surpassing the opposition at its own stylistic level, then challenge it with an alternative design based on modern principles. While this scheme was never put to the test, at its initial attempt the partnership shared third place with Grey Wornum, the architect of the RIBA headquarters building. It must be admitted, *The Architects' Journal* wrote, "that much of the interest of Messrs. Connell, Ward and Lucas's scheme lay in examining how a firm usually so resolutely progressive would react to tiles and brick and stone facings. They do it superbly . . .".[94] "Scandinavian—Romantic—Neo-Classic—Humanistic", commented Astragal in the same issue, "I must retire for awhile and make a major adjustment in my conceptions of architectural standards."[95] The next year, 1936, Connell, Ward and Lucas tried again, entering a neo-Classical design for the Newport Civic Buildings competition, and winning second prize. This their MARS group colleagues would not overlook and called the partners to a meeting to explain their actions. Confronted with laying a charge of wrong-doing, the group discovered that it had never set down any principles or program. To most modern architects, changing one's style to meet the situation suggested a superficiality of artistic involvement that was unacceptable but this was answered by the observation that at such a time the desired end justified the means. After all, Connell was both the Rome Scholar and the architect to design the first, and perhaps the best, modern houses in Britain. Unlike many of his contemporaries who reacted against the academic teaching from which they had to disencumber themselves before attaining a modern style, Connell valued his classical training. As a student he had worked in an embracing discipline which had many virtues except that its symbolism was of a past society. All Connell had to do was to exchange the discipline of the Beaux Arts for that of de Stijl. Having never gone through the pangs of rejection, he had none of the abhorrence of the immediate past that characterized his colleagues. So that while to someone like Fry a return to neo-Georgian would be unthinkable, Connell's idea of bringing conservative patrons up to date by showing them past and present architectural solutions was a reasonable projection from his own experience. Unfortunately, in the year of the end of the Italian conquest of Abyssinia and the beginning of the Spanish Civil War, of Fascist parades through the Jewish district of London and unemployment marches, the belief that the difficulties of popularizing modern architecture could be eased through trickery was as naive as the implied unawareness that the situation had changed since the previous decade. Connell knew that architecture must be an expression of a way of life: he failed to realize that the potency of the classical symbol had been recharged by those who preferred to change society rather than its architecture. The choice between neo-Classic and modern was no longer only between the past and the present, but also between the Fascist present and the democratic present. Both Connell and Lubetkin, who was deeply involved in the censure of his action, remained in the MARS group but took little further interest in its activities.

Unfortunately [wrote Lubetkin about this time for *American Architect and Architecture*] this group has, during the three years of its existence, gradually become less and less of a vital force ... Approaching their problems without much clarity of thought, and having far less in common with one another than they had imagined, these architects have never overcome the initial difficulty of formulating their own definition of modern architecture. In a time of crisis, they might have been able to give more time and attention to the problems of organization and program, but as the whole life of the group has corresponded with a period of specially intense building activity, just those architects who might have made valuable contributions to the group as a whole have been most fully occupied with their own work.* In consequence, the members have been unable to agree on any fundamental issue, and as a result, the volume and importance of their work has been steadily decreasing. A newer organization, which at first sight would appear to have little connection with specifically modern architecture, is the Architects' and Technicians' Organization. This group came together on a purely social and political basis, and is not actually concerned with any stylistic questions, but while its main interest is in such problems as housing, it may perhaps lead to some amelioration of the architect's position. For it is impossible to separate the broader issues of town and regional planning and housing from the whole body of building legislation, and a concentrated attack on this front based on purely utilitarian grounds, might result in a reform of the law and of its administration, which would have important repercussions on the conditions of architectural work. This may seem hard to achieve, but at least it is a far more realistic and promising line of attack than any idealist grouping of modern architects can hope to be.[96]

The ATO however was also having internal problems of policy. With a probable membership peak of around one hundred† (compared to the MARS group seventy in 1937), the ATO was mainly involved with aspects of working class housing. It collaborated with tenants' and owner-occupiers' organizations, preparing reports on defects in old and new properties, explaining developments in planning and housing techniques,

*For example, in 1936 the construction value of public and community buildings was 130 percent above the 1932 level. See Herbert W. Robinson, *The Economics of Building*, London 1939, Appendix 2.

†The ATO figure is taken from a letter to the author from F. Skinner; the MARS group membership for this period is listed in their publication: MARS group, *New Architecture*, London 1938, p. 23.

and sending representatives to meetings and court hearings. Its activities culminated in 1936 with an exhibition designed "to draw attention to the disgraceful conditions of working-class housing to-day"[97] which was shown in London and other cities. Later that year it was invited by the MARS group to work on the next New Homes for Old exhibition, and by the RIBA to submit a report on rehousing to a newly formed committee on housing standards. Its militant socialism which the year before had demanded sanctions against Italy had given way to a milder approach that led a reviewer of the ATO Bulletin to remind the organization that "the only cure for the cancer is the knife".[98] The ATO executive defended its position.

[Some] ATO members and others have seriously thought that the Organisation has concentrated on the social and political obstacles to good architecture to the neglect of the more technical, constructive problems of architecture itself. The Executive Committee, in reply to these criticisms, wishes to stress first that in dealing with housing it was inevitable that a thorough critique should be made both of the vested interests in building and the legislation which helped or retarded the pace and quality of building. The ATO need not therefore apologise for its vigorous excursion into the "political" field. Secondly there was no other organisation at that time capable or prepared to undertake precisely that kind of survey which the ATO thought it necessary to make. However, now that the complacency of certain sections of the community has been slightly punctured and public interest in good housing seems to be re-awakening the ATO believes that it has, to a certain extent, fulfilled its function in that sphere. This is not to say that the ATO will no longer collect information on slum clearance and overcrowding or analyse new legislation. It means that with its limited energies and resources it will tend to concentrate on problems that are more architectural in form and content, leaving the more social and 'political' questions to the various organisations that are growing up to deal with them.[99]

While modern architects debated methods, builders were changing the urban environment. By the end of the nineteen-thirties almost one out of every four dwellings was new, and three quarters of these had been constructed by private enterprise. Architects agitating for the removal of slums and the raising of standards found that their material criticisms were being met by means that ignored their basic design requirements.

Local authorities had been empowered to provide working class dwellings since 1851 and had largely failed to do so. By the nineteen

71

thirties, however, the term 'working class' had lost its precise meaning and, being defined by the 1936 Housing Act as consisting of those who generally earned less than three pounds a week, mainly covered unskilled workers and the substantial unemployed. The majority of wage earners therefore received just too much to qualify for state-aided rental housing and just too little to save sufficient to purchase a house of their own. At the beginning of the decade it had been easy to show that the main part of the population had insufficient capital to benefit from the supply of new houses but as the standard of living increased and hundreds of millions of pounds were spent on betting, drink and tobacco, the arguments became more tenuous. It seemed as if the British working class preferred the immediate stimulation of small luxuries to the long term possibility of better housing. For by 1934 more than three hundred thousand houses were being built each year. Initially helped by subsidies to recover from the effects of the First World War, the private housing industry was then encouraged through the mortgaging system to cater to the growing middle class. Leading the country out of its economic depression, it spilled over into the suburbs and when the higher income groups were satiated, invited the custom of the lower income groups by lowering its deposit requirements and lengthening its terms of repayment. If people were still badly housed it could be argued that it was their own fault. The entrepreneur had found a solution to the problem that did without the services of the modern, or any, architect. The British standard of living was improving by the slow evolution of conservative politics.[100]

As with housing, so with planning. In 1934, a liberal group calling itself the National Housing Committee had voluntarily set about considering a national housing and planning policy. Observing that at Slough, twenty miles west of London, a large industrial estate had been equipped without any housing, and that at Becontree, fifteen miles east of London, a large working class housing estate had been built without any industry, their interim report published in 1936 urged that a central authority be set up to initiate and coordinate local planning projects.

We are fully alive to the dangers inherent in any system of public control over building development and land utilisation . . . But, for good or ill, the country is rapidly passing under the control of the planning schemes of local authorities. Moreover, official action, directly or indirectly, is already constantly interfering with the distribution of industry and population . . . Thus public interference and control are inevitable. The only power that can be relied on to prevent their excessive use is the democratic power of the nation as a whole—a power which is likely, in the long run, to be effective for this purpose . . . We are convinced that a widely effective and wholly beneficial control of industrial location could be exercised, without any compulsion, by well-devised schemes embracing such means as the reservation of convenient and well-equipped industrial sites, the related provision of cheap and efficient transport and public utility services, and firm promises by public authorities to provide, when and where they are needed, adequate and attractive housing, shopping and recreational activities for prospective workers."[101]

The government was also concerned with the problem of planning. While unemployment had greatly decreased since 1932, there still remained a million unemployed, largely evident in a few depressed areas. In 1934 commissioners had been appointed to initiate and aid measures for their economic development and social improvement but little had been achieved. In his report for 1936 at the time of his resignation, the commissioner for England and Wales, Sir Malcolm Stewart, suggested that while industry should not be ordered where to go, there might be good reasons for precluding it from unsatisfactory locations such as London. "It was true", he wrote, "that this would not increase the volume of production but it would secure a better national distribution of industrial activity, and the Special Areas would benefit by obtaining a share of the diverted development."[102] In the middle of the following year, a Royal Commission was set up under Sir Montague Barlow to study the causes, disadvantages and possible reforms of the distribution of the industrial population.

The report of the commission pointed out that while much had been achieved through individuals like Ebenezer Howard, cities such as Liverpool and Manchester, and parliament through its various acts culminating in the Town and Country Planning Act of 1932, the problems of housing and urban planning had not before been studied in their total, national, context. It argued that only at the national level could these problems be solved and that such action is a duty of government. Using the nineteenth century Factory Acts as precedent, invoking the moral image of chain-making women, stripped to the waist, being protected by parliament, the report stated unequivocally that

when conditions affecting the health or well-being rather than the wealth of the State demand attention, when slums, defective sanitation, noise, air pollution and traffic congestion are found to constitute disadvantages, if not dangers, to the community, when the problem,

73

in fact, becomes social in texture rather than economic, then modern civilisation may well require a regulating authority of some kind to step in and take reasonable measures for the protection of the general national interests.[103]

The attitude of industry, the report noted, was apt to be ambivalent. In times of prosperity governmental controls were regarded as interference; during periods of depression government cooperation was not only welcomed but demanded. A city, however, was no longer merely a place of industry but a centre of civilization. So that while industry had proved its philosophy of free enterprise by its own prosperity, there was "a large body of opinion amongst those who can speak from experience and with authority, in favour of *some* regulatory action being taken on national lines and in the national interest".[104]

The commission decided against any major control of industrial location and, after its two years of deliberation, virtually restated the belief that a national board should only have the power to stop new industries from entering the London area. But of its twelve members excluding Barlow, three insisted upon reservations and three submitted a minority report. The reservations were that the national board to be effective must demand whatever powers it needed to carry out the commission's wishes. The minority report, signed by Abercrombie, Elvin and Hichens, set out to show what these powers must be. Professor of civic design at Liverpool University from 1915 to 1935, and then professor of town planning at London University, Patrick Abercrombie was amongst the foremost town planners of his time, later receiving the gold medal of both the RIBA and the American Institute of Architects. In his book *Town and Country Planning*, he had stated the need for a national plan in 1933. The minority report recommended that a new ministry of planning be set up with power to secure a reasonable balance of industrial development throughout the country.

The fact that since 1909 [the minority report stated] there has been an increasing body of legislation on the subject, does not mislead us into supposing that the territorial planning movement is in effective operation from the point of view either of the control exercised or the area covered . . . It is above all becoming apparent that for many purposes the country has to be treated as a single economic unit. Moreover, the State has latterly, by subsidy, by inducement and by negotiation with other countries done much to help particular industries. All this must imply reciprocal responsibilities. A strong and well-balanced industry, a healthy and well-housed population, good educational and recreational facilities, the absence of slums, of poverty and of unemployment are the necessary environment for individual freedom in a well-ordered community . . . The community . . . is in a very real sense a partner in all forms of industrial activity and is entitled both by encouragement and restriction to determine the conditions under which it should operate.[105]

The ministry of planning, in the minority report, would be authorized, with the help of regional advice, to declare in which areas new industries could be set up and would have the necessary funds to encourage them. It would be empowered to purchase land, build trading estates, assist urban development and promote new towns. For

it is important to avoid a facile optimism concerning the prospectus of the nation's health if it be subjected to the risks and hazards of any further degree of unlimited industrial and urban development. To suggest that bad urban conditions are a thing of the past, a mere legacy from the Victorian age which we are rapidly overcoming and need no longer fear, is utterly misleading.[106]

By the end of the nineteen-thirties, the modern architect could claim neither that planning or housing needs were being ignored by a government hostile to the working majority of the people, nor that improvement must necessarily come by revolutionary means. On the contrary it was the MARS group itself that had lost its reforming zeal.

However painstaking MARS were to refute any accusation of stylism [wrote a group of AA students in 1938 criticizing the Burlington House exhibition] . . . they gave no indication of the inter-relation of society, technique and architecture as a constantly moving and changing affair, of the way in which society and technique demands new architectural solutions, and how, when a solution has been achieved, it reacts back on society and technique by indicating the direction for further development and creating new needs. Thus not only was it not made clear how modern architecture arrived at its present stage of development, but also it was not clearly shown that it would develop beyond its present stage. The exhibition merely gave the visitor the impression that MARS would like to see the new architecture applied on a wider scale. Actually, of course, the examination of architecture as something developing in relation to technique and social needs would have involved MARS in a question which as a group they are apparently not willing to face, whatever their opinions may be as individuals. It would have meant their recognition of the obstacles to the proper development of technique inherent in an anachronistic social system; it would, in fact have involved politics . . . Potentially the technique exists for the satisfaction of to-day's immense building needs, but the technical potentialities cannot become actual and cannot be widely applied until society decides to make constructive use of the powers already latent within it. The MARS group, by refusing to face this problem, was forced to escape in its exhibition into formalism.[107]

By this time there were other problems too. In March Germany invaded Austria; in September Chamberlain went to Munich and helped sign away Czechoslovakia's independence. In this atmosphere of fear and indecision, destruction replaced construction as a practical research subject.

It is an odd commentary on a large and intelligent profession [observed a leading article in *The Architects' Journal*] that the slum campaign, ribbon development, trading estates and the rest have not produced any study of the problems involved such as is now produced on Air Raid Precautions by an organization only partially architectural.[108]

The organization was the Association of Architects, Surveyors and Technical Assistants that, under the direction of Cleeve Barr who became its secretary in 1937, had replaced the ATO as the militant centre of activity. Originally established in 1919, it had gained prominence at the end of the nineteen-twenties when it was wooed by the RIBA to support the first Architects' Registration Bill. After a brief period of disillusionment with the RIBA which refused on principle to set a salary scale for private offices to follow, it had rallied to the support of the second Architects' Registration Bill and by the end of the nineteen thirties was represented on various important professional committees. For its report on the design, equipment and cost of air raid shelters, it sent Skinner to Barcelona to gain firsthand experience of aerial bombardment. It did not do much good. For the next few years acrimonious arguments raged over whether deep or surface shelters would be best for a population that needed protection but had to continue working as normally as possible. Tecton published a book on *Planned A.R.P.*[109] based on its underground multi-level design for the London borough of Finsbury and the government ordered trenches to be dug.

We were born into a civilisation whose leaders, whose ideals, whose culture had failed [wrote the AA student editors of *Focus* in the summer of 1938]. They are still in power today. But we, the generation who follow, cannot accept their domination. They lead us always deeper into reaction that we are convinced can only end in disaster.[110]

In 1939 came the first act of catharsis.

6 MILITARY INTERLUDE

The outbreak of war put architects out of work. The building demands of the government's rearmament program which had been initiated in 1936 were met by an industry that had suffered badly in the recent economic depression and wished to add to rather than replace private projects by public contracts. Nevertheless, although private building was not directly restricted until the autumn of 1940, the reduction of conventional commissions greatly affected the employment of architects. Stung by the way that the government negotiated with the building industry without their professional advice being sought, its disregard of the RIBA's offers to help serve the nation and, as a final insult, the haphazard treatment of architecture as a reserved occupation, architects were left to lament that

> In spite of all that the Institute had done for many years to make known to the public the services that only an architect is trained to fulfil, the powers that be have failed to realise his value. They seem unaware that he is anything more than a draughtsman . . .[111]

At the beginning of the war, architects of twenty-five years of age and over were exempted from military service and were only permitted to find employment which utilized their professional qualifications. Theoretically they were to be used in the vast works for the armed forces and industry which kept construction activity at a pre-war level.* The AASTA in a series of publications on evacuation and air raid shelters echoed the editorial statement of *The Architects' Journal* that these tasks were

> a PLANNING problem, depending for efficiency on an organization worked out to the last detail for each administrative area by intelligent whole-time *planners* . . . architects—the professional *planners* . . .[112]

*The number of *employed* insured male workers in the building and civil engineering industries did not fall sharply until 1942: C. M. Kohan, *Works and Buildings*, London 1952, p. 488. See also Central Statistical Office, *Statistical Digest of the War*, London 1951, p. 56.

The government thought otherwise and bypassed architects by giving the work to large contracting firms. The RIBA was in a dilemma, caught between trying to establish the principle of architecture as an essential wartime occupation and altering the law so that its members could earn their livelihood. After a series of moves and countermoves between the government and its advisory committee (at one point of which architectural draftsmen were reserved at a lower age than architects), the profession was removed entirely from the schedule and architects were free to enlist.[113]*

By mid-1940 under Churchill as prime minister, the Labour party had joined the Conservative party in a coalition cabinet and there was little else to do than survive the onrush of the German military. The war became serious and Lord Reith, the celebrated ex-director of the British Broadcasting Corporation, was appointed to a new Department of Works and Buildings and made responsible for the national building program. This was achieved through a series of controls over the direction of men and materials and the location and timing of jobs. The total quantity of building possible was estimated and each government department was allocated a percentage by value (later by labour required) which it was free to use within its own priority system. The information on what resources were available was gathered and processed by a statistical section. All building firms were registered and the necessary trades placed on the schedule of reserved occupations. A more detailed control was effected by designating certain building sites as essential to the war effort and restricting the transfer of operatives from them. So, under the administration of career civil servants and recruited technical experts, the vast building industry was brought under government direction through controls that were mainly still in use at the end of the war when they were available for planned reconstruction.[114]

In the meantime, despite Reith's friendliness towards the architectural profession and the bombing attacks of 1940-1 with their attendant destruction, architects were still considered a luxury and it took considerable persuasion to have them once again, this time fractionally, reserved. And it was not until the end of 1942 that representation was given to the RIBA on the building industry's governmental advisory committee. While many architects found employment in expanded government departments that occupied their time if not their talents, a large number were recruited into the armed forces where the RIBA expended much effort getting them treated as favourably as engineers.

*In this period of indecision, McGrath became a war artist before going to Ireland; Chermayeff left for the USA to lecture and then to teach.

The national government had early recognized the need to include the major representatives of the opposition but the RIBA council maintained itself in office by taking advantage of a wartime act of parliament that gave chartered bodies discretionary permission to suspend annual elections. At the same time it sought to attune its activities to the communal sense of purpose that had come with adversity. As a commentator in the RIBA *Journal* had remarked on the Barlow report at the beginning of 1940:

If the majority's recommendation can be said roughly to represent what parliamentary and public opinion might have been expected to accept two and a half years ago (when the Commissioners were beginning their labours), and the first minority's recommendations what they would have accepted just before the outbreak of war, the views of the second minority [Abercrombie's proposals] may perhaps be reckoned a fairly shrewd anticipation of the measures our democracy may be ready to adopt when the war is over.[115]

The equalitarianism of air raids and rationing brought unity of purpose and was encouraged by the government. As Reith said in parliament:

I am sure that the idea of a planned and ordered reconstruction is an incentive to and encouragement of war effort, and in fact a high and worthy war purpose itself.[116]

The RIBA took the minister's statements seriously. At the beginning of the war a committee of three—Robertson, Duncan and Goodhart-Rendel—had been appointed to advise on the current and future use of the profession. As few commissions were available it suggested carrying out research into prevailing problems. This idea was then expanded into a Reconstruction Committee which came into being in the spring of 1941 "to consider and formulate the policy of the RIBA and the Allied Societies on the subject of post-war reconstruction and planning."[117] With Robertson as chairman of its policy group, the main committee consisted of a spectrum of opinion from the venerable Sir Banister Fletcher to the youthful Ralph Tubbs. Its reports, which by its constitution were collative rather than original, touched upon the subjects of planning, housing, law, the building industry and the profession* and were largely drawn up as submissions to the govern-

---

*Its reports were on: planning and amenities, wartime housing, law and building structure, reconstruction and the architectural profession, legislation affecting town and country planning, the capacities of the building industry, rationalization of building legislation, town and country planning. These were published in the RIBA *Journal* in the period 1941–45. A further report on housing was published separately in 1944.

ILLUSTRATIONS

Most architectural photographs are taken in patiently awaited sunshine, without people, in static views that carefully exclude unwanted details. The reality is both more vital and ordinary. Several of the buildings illustrated have been altered by time or their owners – even the Royal Festival Hall. Some such as Sassoon House were in poor condition when visited; many were shoddy like the Finsbury Health Centre. Checkley's Cambridge house was divided into apartments; the Impington Village College added to. Others naturally retain (Peter Jones store) or are maintained in (New Farm) the pristine state that first projected them into architectural importance.

Above: Ludwig Mies van der Rohe *et al*. Weissenhof Exhibition, Stuttgart, Germany. 1
Below: Peter Behrens. House, Northampton. 1926.

Above: Easton and Robertson. Royal Horticultural Society Exhibition Hall, London. 1928. Left: Thomas Tait. House Silver End, Essex. 1927. Buildings such as these and Arnos Grove Underground Station (page 92) presented a comfortable stylistic alternative that was quashed by the critical success of the International Style.

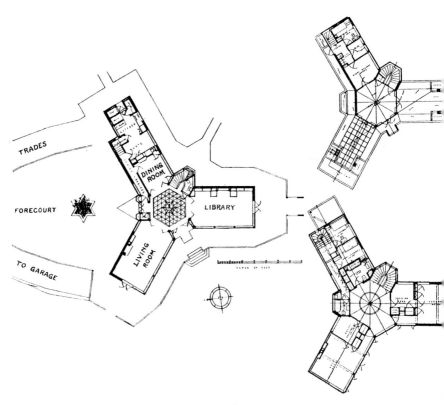

TRADES

FORECOURT

TO GARAGE

DINING ROOM

LIBRARY

LIVING ROOM

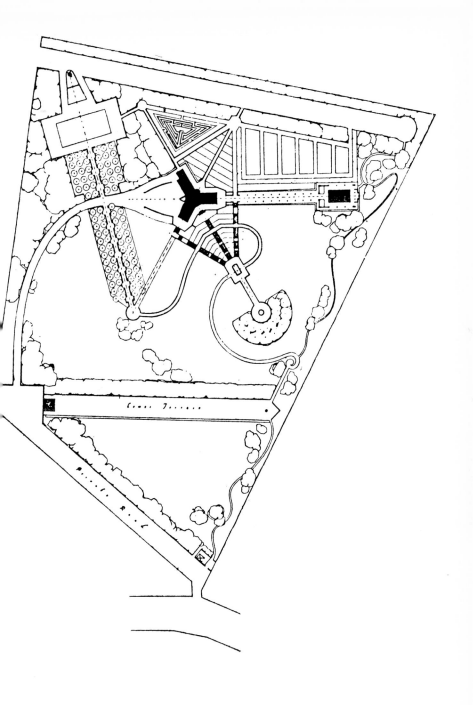

e, and facing: Amyas Connell. High and Over, Amersham, Bucks. 1930. The first
uivocally modern exterior, it was designed 1928-9 when Connell was twenty-seven
old. Above: Landscape plan.

85

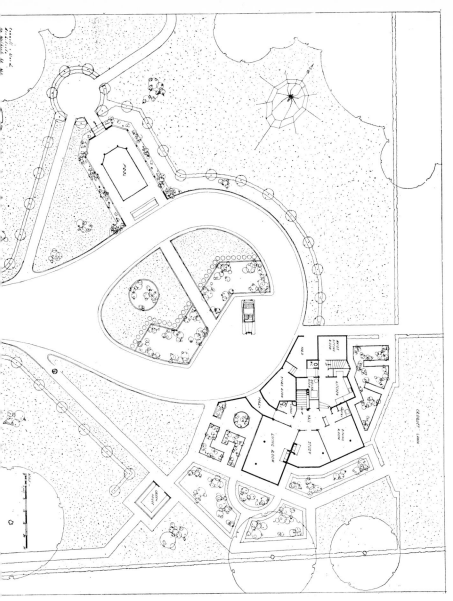

Right and facing: Amyas Connell. New Farm, Haslemere, Surrey. 1932. Note from the plan the columns in the main rooms cluttering up the living space.

Joseph Emberton. Royal Corinthian Yacht Club, Burnham-on-Crouch, Essex. 1931.

Owen Williams. Boots Factory, Nottingham. 1931.

Above: Owen Williams. Pioneer Health Centre, London. 1935. Located adjacent to Sass House (page 100), the individualistic robustness of the Health Centre design can be compared to Sassoon House's typical carton rectangularity. Below: George Checkley. Ho Cambridge. 1931.

Connell and Ward. Houses, Ruislip, Middlesex. 1935. In their stark modernity the *cause célèbre* of the early 1930s, the houses were later surrounded and subdued by the spread of London's suburbs.

Colin Lucas. The Hopfield, Wrotham, Kent. 1933.

Above: Charles Holden *et al.* Arnos Grove Underground Station, London. 1932.

Below: Tecton. Penguin Pool, London. 1934. A 4000 square feet oasis (370 m²) in Regen
Park zoo, its interior provided a peepshow of the shape of things to come.

Tecton. Highpoint One, London. 1935. See also overleaf.

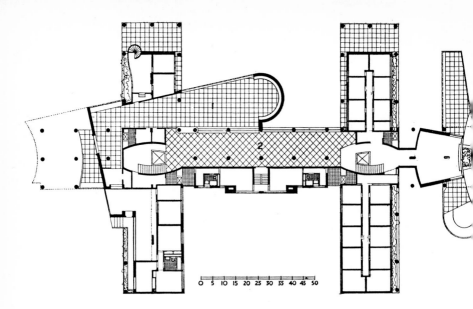

Above: Highpoint One, entrance floor plan. The main hall is reached longitudinally from
oblique entry and extends through the second elevator lobby to a tea room overlooking 1
garden. Facing: Highpoint One, analytical studies.

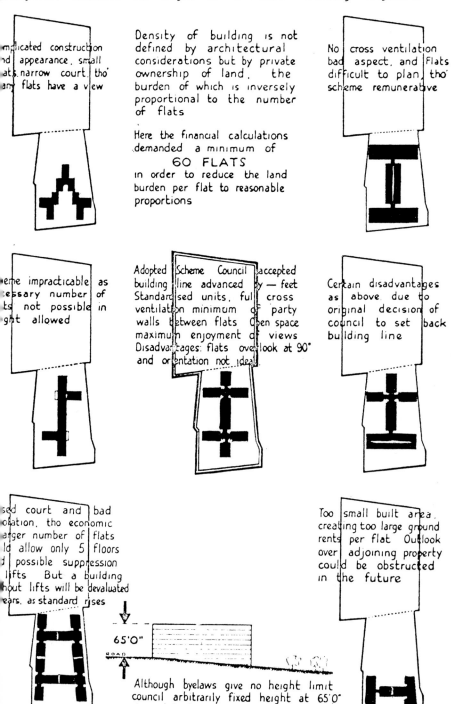

d permanent open spaces. instead of allowing a high building the council.
ortsightedly restricted the height to 6 floors creating congestion

mplicated construction
nd appearance. small
ats narrow court. tho'
any flats have a view

Density of building is not
defined by architectural
considerations but by private
ownership of land. the
burden of which is inversely
proportional to the number
of flats

No cross ventilation
bad aspect. and Flats
difficult to plan, tho'
scheme remunerative

Here the financial calculations
demanded a minimum of
60 FLATS
in order to reduce the land
burden per flat to reasonable
proportions

eme impracticable as
cessary number of
ts not possible in
ght allowed

Adopted Scheme Council accepted
building line advanced by — feet
Standardised units, full cross
ventilation minimum of party
walls between flats Open space
maximum enjoyment of views
Disadvantages: flats overlook at 90°
and orientation not ideal

Certain disadvantages
as above. due to
original decision of
council to set back
building line

sed court and bad
otation. tho economic
arger number of flats
ld allow only 5 floors
d possible suppression
lifts But a building
hout lifts will be devaluated
ears. as standard rises

Too small built area.
creating too large ground
rents per flat. Outlook
over adjoining property
could be obstructed
in the future

65'0"

Although byelaws give no height limit
council arbitrarily fixed height at 65'0"
at road front but gave no limit at back

95

ve: Tecton. Finsbury Health Centre, London. 1938. The functional articulation and osition of this building, and its surface composition, can be compared with Lasdun's t-war cluster blocks (page 145) both in their intellectual rationalizations and pictorial inerisms.

cing, top: Tecton. Highpoint Two, London. 1938. Garden front. Facing, bottom: High-nt Two, entrance. The confusion of brick, concrete, glass block and tile surrounding famous entrance caryatids, contrasts with the composed simplicity of the garden facade.

Connell, Ward and Lucas. House, London. 1938. Building permission was opposed by
local authority (as well as by other architects) even though Fry's Sun House (page
top) had been completed just a little way up the road. 'Connell, Ward and Lucas are
trouble again', commented Astragal.

William Crabtree *et al*. Peter Jones Store, London. 1939.

Above: Sassoon House, London. 1934 (photo 1955). Committed to a single comprehensi style, the modern architect such as Fry used the same elements for low-income apartm like Sassoon House in the city as he did for luxurious houses like that at Kingston in suburbs (page 102). The low capacity of some of these buildings to withstand the weathe of London's climate and their relatively high cost of maintenance has often resulted in t standing for years in a dilapidated condition until refurbished. Below: Sassoon Ho entrance front. (Photo 1934.)

Above: E. Maxwell Fry. Sun House, London. 1936.

Left: E. Maxwell Fry *et al.* Kensal House, London. 1936.

E. Maxwell Fry House Kingston Surrey 1937

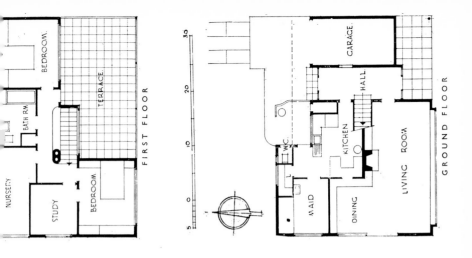

BEDROOM.

NURSERY

BATH RM

STUDY

TERRACE.

BEDROOM

FIRST FLOOR

GARAGE.

WC

HALL

KITCHEN

MAID

DINING

LIVING ROOM

GROUND FLOOR

This page: F. R. S. Yorke. House, Iver, Bucks. 1936. Typical in its fussiness, the building uses seventeen outside vertical angles to house a set of conventional rooms.

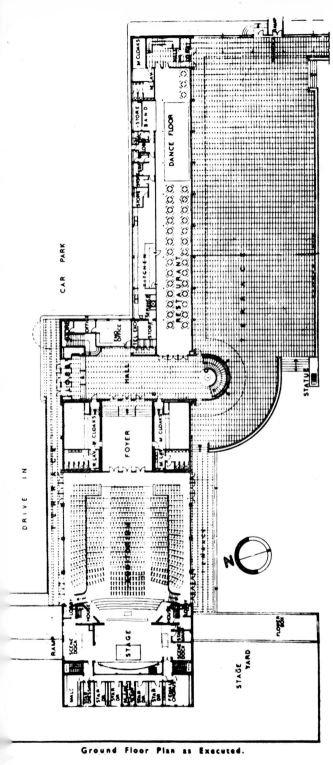

Ground Floor Plan as Executed.

DRIVE IN

CAR PARK

N

RAMP

SCENE DOCK

STAGE

STAGE YARD

FOYER

HALL

DANCE FLOOR

RESTAURANT

TERRACE

STATUE

Top of facing page: Gropius and Fry, Mendelsohn and Chermayeff. Houses, London. 1936. The buildings are constructed of brick. Bottom of facing page: Mendelsohn and Chermayeff. De La Warr Pavilion, Bexhill, Sussex. 1935. When a member of the British Union of Fascists wrote condemning the use of an alien architect, De la Warr, then mayor, replied quoting the RIBA that if Mendelsohn stayed and applied for naturalization, 'they would be pleased and proud to consider him for the bestowal of the highest honours that the profession could give'. See also next page.

De La Warr Pavilion, stair leading down to entrance hall.

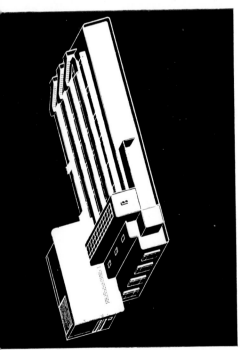

Above and left: Wells Coates.
Lawn Road Flats, London. 1934.
Although the entrance front faces
east, the sun seldom shines as often
as the architect intended. According
to the owner, the original cement
wash was too costly to maintain.

Right and facing page: Gropius and
Fry. Village College, Impington,
Cambridgeshire. 1939. The
commonplace exterior covers a
plan that lacks a spatial relationship
between circulation and rooms but
presages the informality that
characterized the design of the
post-war schools.

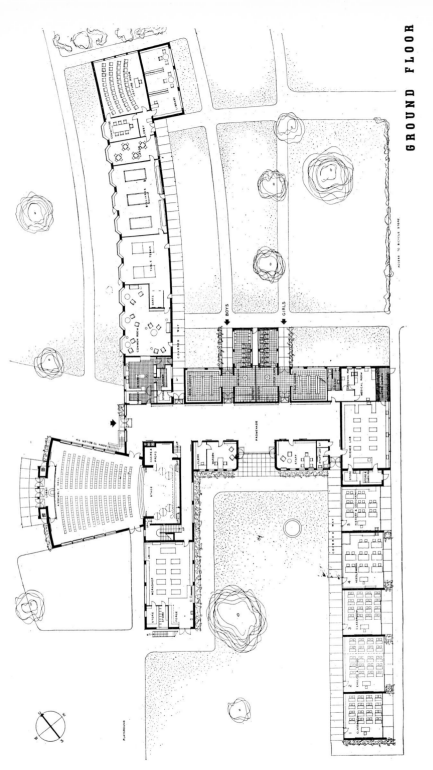

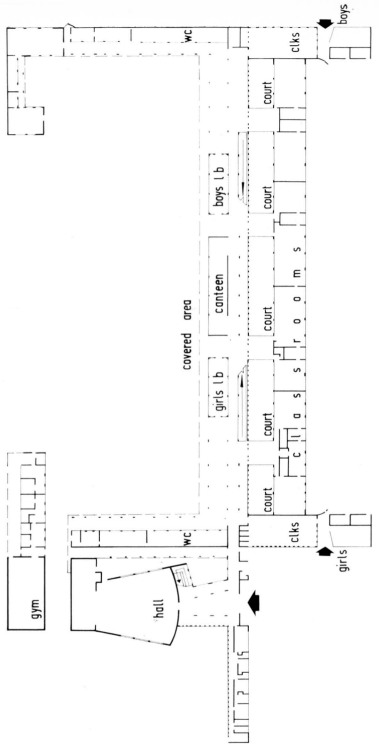

Denis Clarke Hall. School, *News Chronicle* Competition. 1937. The Bauhaus-type elementarism of the preceding decade, seen in Clarke Hall's prizewinning plan, was favoured by MARS group architects even though discarded by their mentor, Gropius (Page 109).

ell, Ward and Lucas. Kent House, London. 1935. The International Style gained its
through black and white photogeneity before the invention of colour film. Kent House
ink walls and bright red balconies.

Above and below: Connell, Ward and Lucas. Newport Civic Buildings Competition.
Called before the MARS group to explain their behaviour, Connell and Ward (on their
to a reception) appeared in evening dress, which further offended Lubetkin's principles.

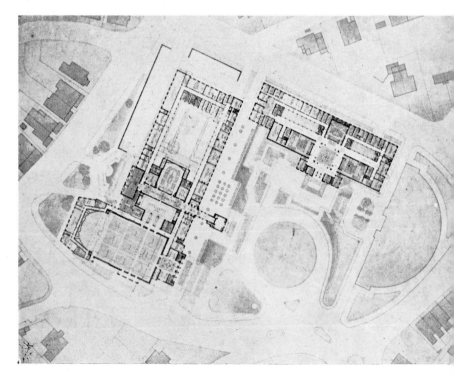

Private Enterprise Housing, London. 1930s.

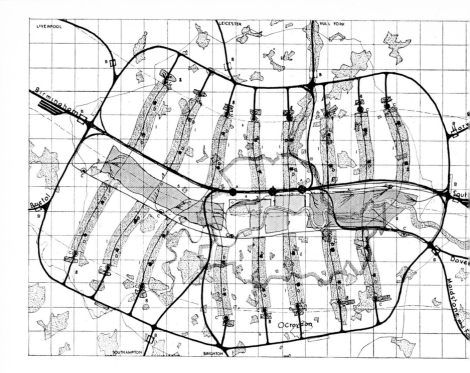

MARS group. London Reconstruction Project. 1942. Conceived before the war, it was p
licized in *The Architectural Review* after bombing and hopes for a bright new world
made such projects fashionable. There will be work enough, quoted Astragal, 'without
proposals to sweep away a whole city (together with its history, local associations
millions of pounds worth of underground services) and rebuild it in endless vistas of
glass and parkland'.

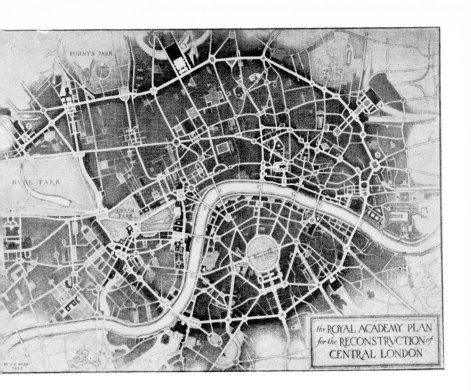

Above and below: Royal Academy. London Reconstruction Project. 1942

Above: London Regional Reconstruction Committee. London Reconstruction Project. 1
Below: J. H. Forshaw and Patrick Abercrombie. County of London Plan. 1943.

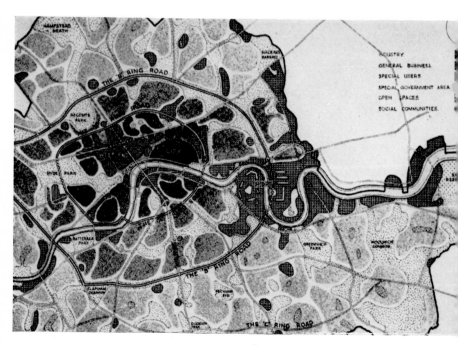

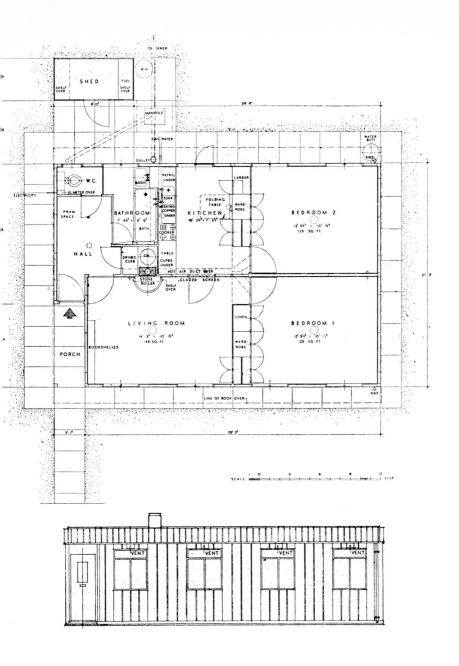

This page: Ministry of Works. Portal House. 1944. Churchill, in a nationwide radio talk, announced the future production of half a million temporary houses. Nine months later the Portal program was cancelled and help was solicited from the USA. 8462 dwellings were delivered on lend-lease. The British supplied 148,205 more.

Jackson and Edmunds. Crystal Palace Competition. 1946.

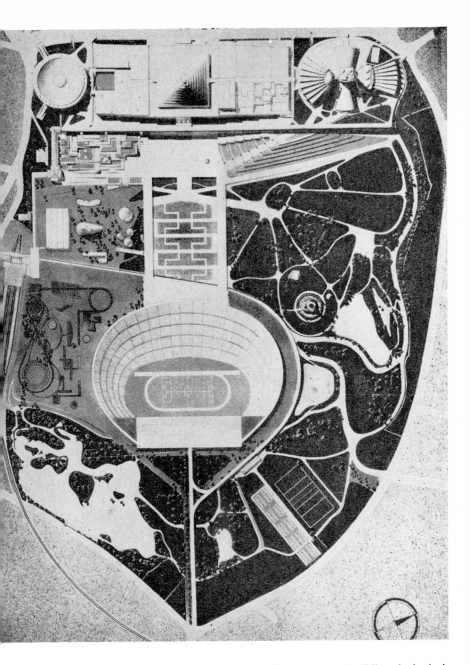

...twistle and Arup. Crystal Palace Competition. 1946. 'The functional buildings look nice', ...mmented Kenneth Clark, 'but they do not fulfil their functions, while those on *beaux* ...*s* lines do not look so nice but are exceedingly functional.'

Public Authority Housing, London. 1940s.

Facing page, top: Tecton. Spa Green Estate, London. 1949. 'For too long modern archi‐
tural solutions were regarded in terms of abstract principles, with formal expression
to itself as a functional resultant. The principles of composition, the emotional impact of
visual, were brushed aside as irrelevant. Yet this is the very material with which the archi‐
operates; it is in this sphere that he is the sole master, by virtue of his training and traditic
(Lubetkin, 1951.) Facing page, bottom: Norman and Dawbarn. St. Pancras Way, Lond
1949.

Powell and Moya. Churchill Gardens, London. 1948–. Success for the young post-graduate was actually building what his teachers had envisioned.

Above: Temporary Prefabricated Housing, 1945–7. The three main units supplied were the Aluminium (54,500), the Arcon (39,000), and the Uni-Seco (29,000) here shown in use twenty years later. Though their manufactured look seemed more in keeping with the new technological era than that of conventional housing, they averaged out over £100 more than the ordinary three-bedroom house. Below: Ministry of Works, Standardized School Construction. 1944.

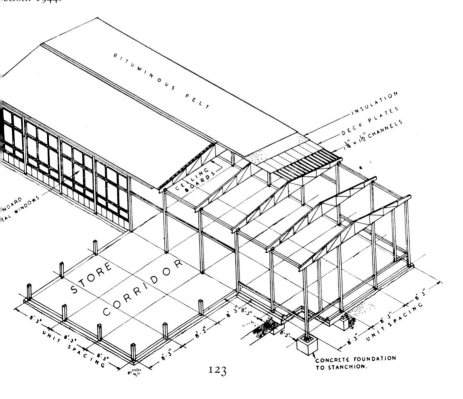

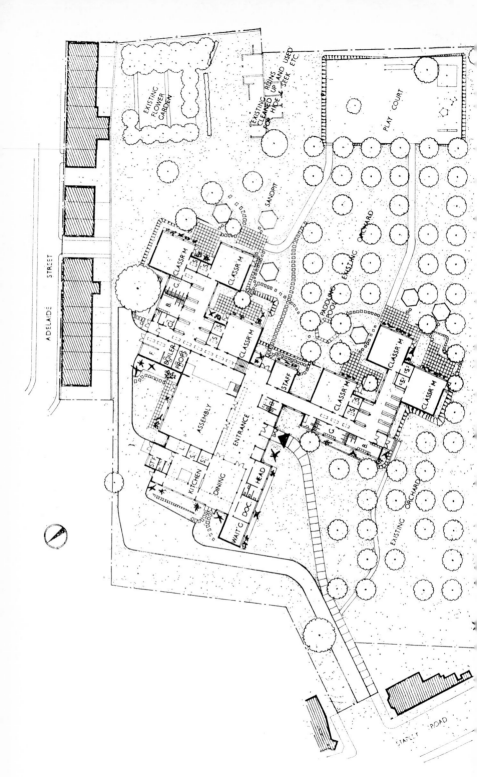

ADELAIDE STREET

EXISTING
FLOWER
GARDEN

EXISTING RUINS
CLEANED UP AND USED
FOR HIDE & SEEK ETC.

PLAY COURT

SANDPIT

EXISTING ORCHARD

PADDLING
POOL

CLASS'R M
3S′

CLASS'R M

CLASS'R M

CLASS'R M
3S′

B.
CLS.

CLASS'R M
3S′

CLASS'R M
3S′ 3S′

CLASS'R M

STAFF

CLASS'R M
3S′ 3S′

CLASS'R M
3S′ 3S′

BOILER
PROB'S

F.

ASSEMBLY

ENTRANCE

STF.
S.

KITCHEN

DINING

HEAD

WAIT'G DOC

EXISTING ORCHARD

STAPLEY ROAD

124

Right and facing page:
Hertfordshire County Council.
Aboyne Lodge School, St. Albans,
Herts. 1949.

Above and facing page: Hertfordshire County Council, Templewood School, Welwyn, Herts, 1949.

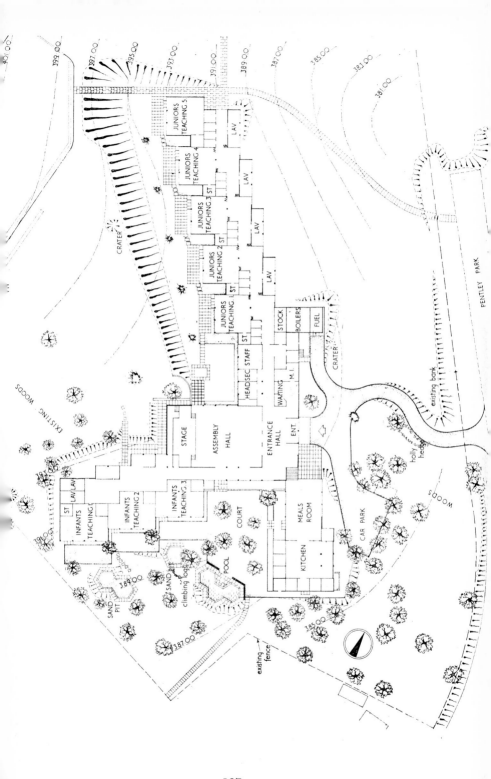

128

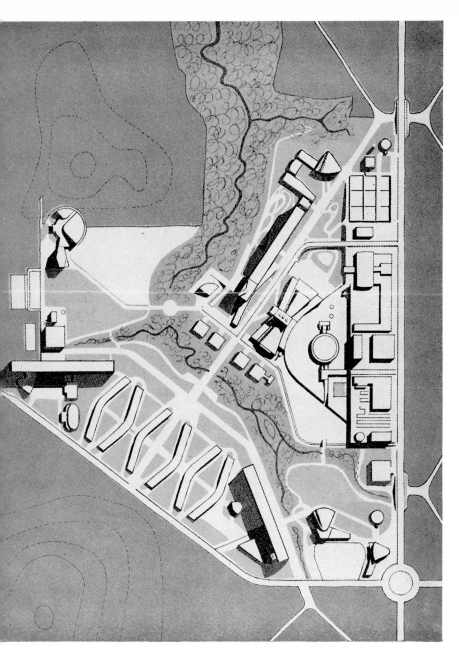

Facing page:
Frederick Gibberd
et al. Harlow New
Town, Essex.
1948–. The photo-
graph of the town
was taken ten
years after its
designation.
Right: Berthold
Lubetkin.
Peterlee, Durham.
1950.

129

Above and facing page: Hugh Casson *et al*. Festival of Britain, London. 1951. Drinking
under the trees, the visitor could imagine himself on the Continent.

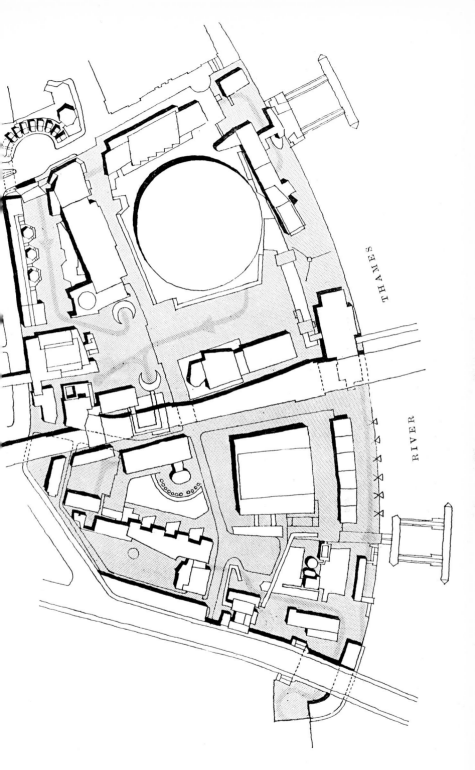

THAMES

RIVER

Above: Ralph Tubbs. Dome of Discovery, London. 1951. Below: Frederick Gibb Lansbury Market Centre, London. 1951. Like other post-war buildings in a vernac style, no matter how sensible (page 121, bottom), Lansbury failed to provide a new loc match the spirit of a new way of life.

Above and left:
London County
Council. Royal
Festival Hall,
London. 1951.
Half the young
architects who
detailed the build-
ing were graduates
of the Regent
Street Polytechnic
where Peter Moro
had previously
taught.
Left, foyer.

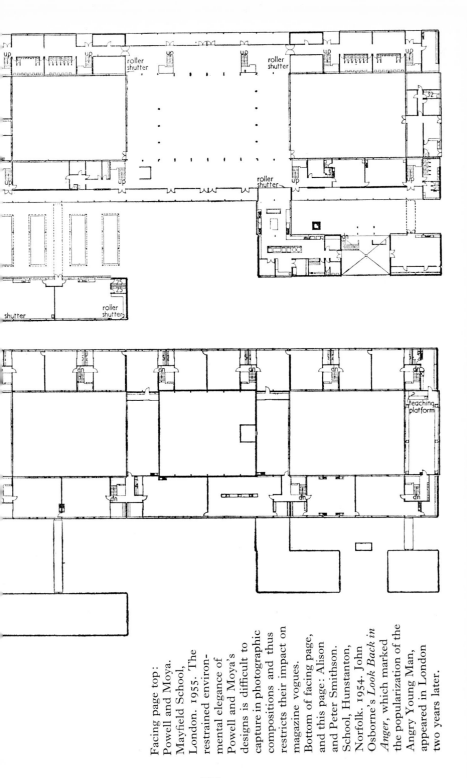

Facing page top: Powell and Moya. Mayfield School, London. 1955. The restrained environmental elegance of Powell and Moya's designs is difficult to capture in photographic compositions and thus restricts their impact on magazine vogues. Bottom of facing page, and this page: Alison and Peter Smithson. School, Hunstanton, Norfolk. 1954. John Osborne's *Look Back in Anger*, which marked the popularization of the Angry Young Man, appeared in London two years later.

Alison and Peter Smithson. Economist Building, London. 1964.

op of facing page: Alison and Peter Smithson. Housing, Golden Lane Competition. 1952.
acing page, bottom: London County Council. Alton Estate East, London. 1955.

Above, and top of facing page: London County Council. Alton Estate West, London. 195
Below, and bottom of facing page: Stirling and Gowan. Langham House Close, Ham Comon, Surrey. 1958. The rough aesthetic was carried into the interior and Stirling observ
later that he was a bit disillusioned when tenants had their fireplaces plastered.

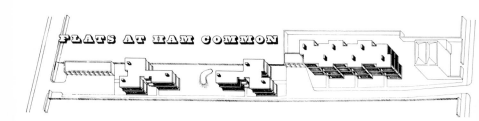

FLATS AT HAM COMMON

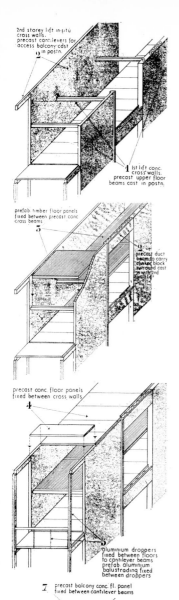

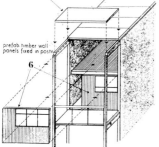

Labels on constructional details:

2nd storey lift in-situ cross walls. precast cantilevers for access balcony cast in postn. **1**

1st lift conc. cross walls. precast upper floor beams cast in postn. **2**

prefab. timber floor panels fixed between precast conc. cross beams **3**

precast duct beam to carry clinker block surround cast in with 2nd

precast conc. floor panels fixed between cross walls **4**

aluminium droppers fixed between floors to cantilever beams prefab. aluminium balustrading fixed between droppers **5**

precast balcony conc. fl. panel fixed between cantilever beams **7**

prefab. timber wall panels fixed in postn. **6**

This page: London County Council. Elmington Estate, London. 1957. Top: under construction. Left: constructional details.

Facing page: Sheffield City Council. Park Hill, Sheffield. 1961. The term 'working class' which included mechanics, artisans, labourers, hawkers and costermongers, was rejected by the courts in 1948 as being 'quite inappropriate to modern social condition It would be difficult to claim, however, that the conce of 'working class housing' was thereby removed from the minds of architects and building authorities.

140

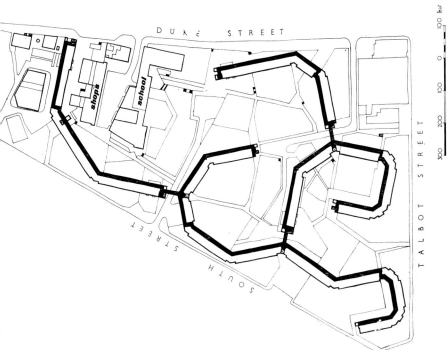

Left: Eric Lyon
Parkleys
Richmond,
Surrey. 1956.

Below: Ministry
of Housing et al
St. Mary's Esta
Oldham. 1967.
One of the recen
improved housin
estates.

Chamberlin, Powell and Bon. Trinity School, London. 1960.

This page: Denys Lasdun.
Cluster block, London.
1959 (designed 1955).

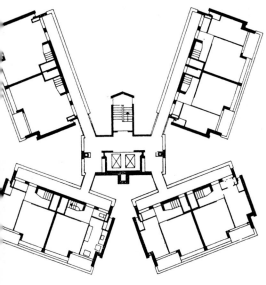

Facing page: Drake and
Lasdun. Hallfield School,
London. 1955 (designed
1951).

Denys Lasdun. Apartment building, London. 1960 (designed 1958).

This page: Denys Lasdun.
Royal College of Physicians,
London. 1964 (designed 1960).

Above: Architects' Co-Partnership. Dunelm House, University of Durham. 1966. Be
Ahrends, Burton and Koralek. Theological College, Chichester. 1965. Two example
design sophistication in the 1960s after half a century of an international modern styl

...on and Conder. Arts Faculties, Cambridge University. 1959–. Like the work of Easton Robertson a generation earlier, this group of buildings was too eclectic to influence the ...ic pattern of construction on expanding campuses (see page 160 bottom, for its neighbour.

149

This page: Stirling and Gowan. Engineering Building, University of Leicester. 1963. Fa
page: Nottinghamshire County Council. Rushcliffe School, West Bridgeford. 196
typical CLASP school. (see also next page).

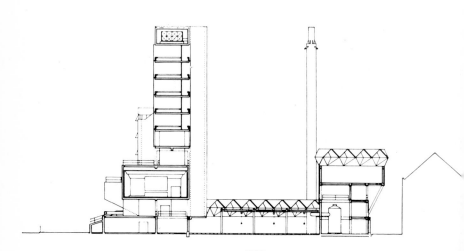

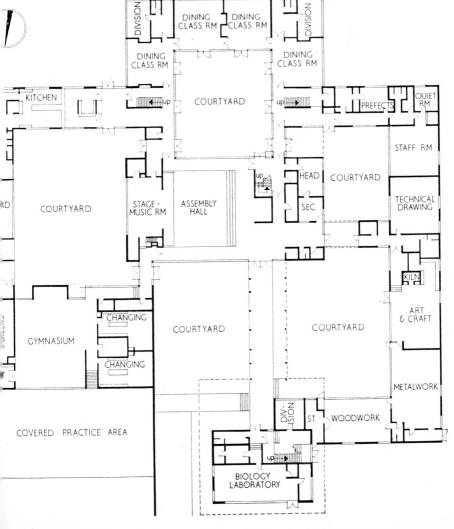

DIVISION

DINING
CLASS RM

DINING
CLASS RM

DIVISION

DINING
CLASS RM

DINING
CLASS RM

KITCHEN

up

COURTYARD

up

PREFECTS

QUIET
RM

STAFF RM

COURTYARD

STAGE -
MUSIC RM

ASSEMBLY
HALL

up

HEAD

SEC.

COURTYARD

TECHNICAL
DRAWING

KILN

CHANGING

GYMNASIUM

COURTYARD

COURTYARD

ART
& CRAFT

CHANGING

DIV-
ISION

ST.

WOODWORK

METALWORK

COVERED PRACTICE AREA

up

BIOLOGY
LABORATORY

Above and left: Coventry City Council. John F. Kennedy School, Coventry. 1967. A later and more lavish CLASP school.

Matthew, Johnson-Marshall. University of York. 1965–. See also next page.

University of York. Aerial view.

Above: Stevenage
Development
Corporation.
Town Centre,
Stevenage. 1958–.

Left: Coventry
City Council.
City Centre,
Coventry. 1948–.
Although its
design falls below
the connoisseur's
standard of good
taste, Coventry's
city centre has a
social vitality that
others lack.

This page: London County Council. Hook New Town Project. 1960.

North

open space

open space

Cumbernauld Development Corporation. Cumbernauld New Town. 1958–. For the 55 per cent of the population who walk to the town centre, there is some discrepancy between the journeys through the rain and the covered shopping in between. Perhaps its intended 5000 parking spaces will become occupied as car ownership increases—though by that time people might be looking for more spacious housing. See also next page.

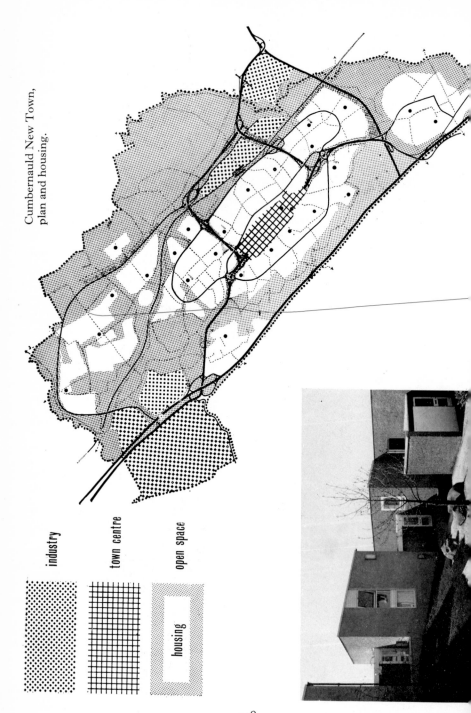

Cumbernauld New Town, plan and housing.

industry

town centre

open space

housing

Denys Lasdun. University of East Anglia, Norwich. 1966– (designed 1962–8).

Above: London
County Council
Arts Centre,
London. 196

Left:
James Stirlir
History Facu
Building,
Cambridge
University. 1

ment. On social, economic, legal and technical questions which were mainly outside the RIBA's jurisdiction, its comments were well-meaning and somewhat naive, expressing the general belief that everything else should be better controlled. On its own architectural problems of training, organization and practice, the Reconstruction Committee was virtuously silent. Its enthusiasm culminated in the first half of 1943 with two exhibitions at the National Gallery, one On Rebuilding Britain and the other presenting a master plan for London. By this time internal dissensions were occupying the thoughts of other members.

The RIBA council had two blocks of representatives, one nominated by the Allied Societies in the United Kingdom, excluding London, and the other elected by the national membership. Being parochial, the former was inherently conservative; the latter, with its wider representation, more accurately reflected the tastes of the profession. The RIBA council of 1939 had been overwhelmingly conventional. At first there was little objection to its continuing in office but as the course of the war improved and thoughts turned to the promise of a new post-war life, agitation began against an administration associated with the disillusionment of pre-war years. Through 1942 and 1943 the arguments for holding elections, initiated by MARS group members and backed by petitions and the editors of The Architects' Journal, were disdainfully rejected by Sir Ian MacAlister who had been RIBA secretary for over thirty years, but shortly after his retirement an election was announced in 1944. The AASTA, renamed the Association of Building Technicians, which had profited from the prevalent reforming zeal to increase its membership to a quarter of the RIBA's,* repeated its previous election record of getting six of its nominees elected. However, the success of this London based movement in exorcizing the spectre of traditionalism was far from complete when at the head of the national voting count was an RIBA council appointee of the gothic/classic school.

The national concern with the growth of London as expressed in the Barlow report and the incentive to rebuild given by the devastation of bombing, induced a number of organizations to use the capital as the symbol of post-war reconstruction. The first proposal for its future

*The membership figures of the ABT (which became a member of the Trades Union Congress in 1941) were repeatedly quoted in its magazine Keystone during its membership drive and reached over two thousand during 1942. Although architects formed only one section of the ABT, there were also sympathizers who were honorary members and these included such persons as Carter, Lubetkin, Martin and Summerson. See also John Summerson, "Bread & butter and architecture", Horizon, VI, 1942, pp. 233–243.

L

development was presented by the MARS group. Under the chairmanship of Arthur Korn,[118] an ex-member of the German *Ring* who had been in Britain since 1937, and with the help of Samuely on transportation and finance, its town planning committee redesigned London in its entirety with that utopian disregard of the vagaries of society previously popularized by Le Corbusier. Their plan for reorganizing the structure of London into parallel districts separated by parks and feeding into central linear industrial zones on either side of a purified existing metropolitan core, completely overlooked the fact that a society that would rehabilitate itself so comprehensively was not a society that would have got itself into that state in the first place. Even their fellow MARS group members were rather shocked.

Bemused by the general's bold arrows on the map [wrote Lionel Brett in *The Architects' Journal*], deafened by his barrage of statistics, we all begin to cheer. But the map is put aside, the barrage dies away and we are left feeling the battle has yet to be fought. . . In the field of planning, we have to re-integrate communities and functions much as MARS proposes, but making, I suggest, a much more sensitive use of what exists. . . How much richer the mind's life in an old city thus purged and renewed than in the Martian utopia . . . Can we not therefore, before some of the best architectural brains go searching for their geometrical stars, grab their coat-tails and induce them to tackle the far subtler problems which in their absence, as so often before, lesser men may mishandle?[119]

Such attempts were not long in coming. The same year the Royal Academy presented its Beaux Arts plan backed by the aristocracy of the profession, and a year later the RIBA published its proposals which had been worked out by a committee drawn from its second rank of senior members. The insipid decomposition of London that it suggested was shortly afterwards forgotten with the previous plans of revolution and reaction in general admiration of the official designs of the London County Council.

The MARS Group desires to convey to the London County Council its welcome of the County of London Plan as the first adequate and comprehensive plan for the county and one of the first plans to be sponsored by an official body, in which modern planning principles are applied to an established social organism. As you may be aware, the MARS Group has been concerned with the study of London Planning for a number of years, and the results of its researches have been the subject of public notice from time to time. These researches have necessarily been on the theoretical plane, and it has given great satisfaction to the Group to see some of the principles which it adopted worked out in a full context of factual information.[120]

The RIBA was also pleased to share its achievements with the official plan.

> Now the L.C.C. plan is before the public [wrote the RIBA president to *The Times*] it is interesting to compare it with the London Regional Reconstruction Committee plan which is now on exhibition at the National Gallery and to observe that the same broad principles exist in each scheme.[121]

Produced by Abercrombie and Forshaw, now chief architect to the London County Council, the County of London plan proposed its rehabilitation by easing its traffic congestion, replacing its slums, disentangling incompatible building uses and providing open spaces where required.[122]

The plan had been requested by Reith as part of his duties to consult with others and advise the government on the methods and means of the post-war reconstruction of towns and country. Unfortunately these wide terms of reference were narrowed by the subsequent formation of the ministries of Town and Country Planning and Reconstruction, and the responsibility of the Ministry of Works was reduced to the more technical aspects of post-war building policy. This was executed through the Directorate of Post-War Building and its attendant committees for Standards and Codes of Practice which, by combining the expertise of individuals and institutions with their own organization, made the insular program of the RIBA irrelevant. Their activity absorbed the services of many architects with Scott and Wornum as chairmen of policy committees and Towndrow as Controller of Experimental Building Development. From 1944 on a stream of reports set out the basic criteria for future building. Appointed by government departments or convened by research associations, trade federations and professional institutions (including the RIBA), the committees represented the views of specialists in many fields. But these reports were merely advisory with the government carefully disclaiming any commitment, and recommendations, however excellent, to be effective require political action.

Although the Conservative party had initiated the Barlow commission and supported the Scott and Uthwatt commissions called by Reith to inquire into the utilization of land in rural areas and compensation and betterment, it really had little interest in comprehensive planning and while the war lasted was content to let future social improvements remain topics for inspiriting discussion. When the government did act the result could be ironic. It was evident that the building industry had been disrupted by the war and that traditional building materials would be in short supply. With the obvious need for unlimited housing, the Labour party wished to concentrate on permanent construction, the Conservative party to use industrial methods to supply immediate temporary units.

> I hope we may make up to half a million of these [Churchill told the nation] . . . The whole business is to be treated as a military evolution . . . As much thought has been and will be put into this plan as was put into the invasion of Africa . . .[123]

Designed through the Ministry of Works and named after its minister, the steel Portal house, which was intended to roll off the assembly lines that had hitherto been mass producing articles of war, was unveiled at the Tate Gallery in London in the middle of 1944. The architectural reaction was hostile to the awkward design of this minimal dwelling and all through the summer *The Architects' Journal* published correspondents' plans to show how it could be improved. To appease its critics the ministry also tried again but the result was just as unacceptable as before.

> As was feared [wrote Astragal], the Revised Version of the Portal House with its inexcusably bad plan has been accepted . . . Surely some notice could have been taken of the many excellent suggestions on revised plans which were published in the technical Press . . .[124]

The lament was premature. One month later a new Minister of Works announced the cancellation of the program. The continuing war left no steel for its production.

The Labour party's policy towards matters affecting post-war architecture was ostensibly more enlightened. It recognized the need for immediate preparatory measures in readiness for the huge building program contemplated and proposed that not only should surveyors, architects, engineers and planners be released from the military, but that the training of such professionals should be treated as a reserved occupation. Yet it was one of the Labour party's leaders, Ernest Bevin, who as Minister of Labour and National Service in the coalition government, refused the early release of architects saying that he was not going to let any profession intimidate him into letting its members home before the common serving man.[125]

The attitude of the Conservative party to the reconstruction program it offered when the people were being asked to make a supreme effort to avoid defeat was summed up in a political speech by Churchill when he stated that recovery would only be achieved by once again flying the flag of free enterprise. The Labour party had no intention of continuing a coalition into peacetime and forced a parliamentary election by withdrawing from the government. The Conservative party looked back to a successfully completed war and the belief that only they were fit to govern. The Labour party's appeal was planning: "Years of chaos and mismanagement . . . end on the beaches of Dunkirk. Months of careful planning . . . lead to D-day." Promising to continue by legislation the voluntary equalitarianism engendered by the war, the Labour party gained an overwhelming majority and, ushering in the post-war era, opened parliament with the singing of The Red Flag.

7 PUBLIC SERVICE

The physical environment was worn and damaged. With a shortage of labour and materials, the government planned its renewal. Through conscription and employment in other more essential industries, the building labour force had shrunk to a third of its pre-war size. All materials and components were in short supply. Factories were changing over from military production and there was little money available to buy from foreign markets. The building program was incalculable.

Two hundred thousand houses had been destroyed, a quarter of a million made uninhabitable, and an even larger number were in need of repair. Added to these were the unending normal requirements for the replacement of slum and the raising of standards that had been neglected in the five preceding years. Rejecting any specific targets for house construction, the government promised to build as many as was feasible within the economy. By 1948 the annual output was around two hundred thousand. Of these less than one fifth was by private enterprise in contrast to its pre-war record of over a quarter of a million each year.

The Labour government argued that private enterprise, building for profit, could only satisfy the demands of the middle income group; to house the lower income group it was necessary to provide rental dwellings as a public service. The division of responsibility had previously been a cause of social segregation. The 1949 Housing Act, deleting references to the working classes, a term which was already legally unacceptable, made local authorities responsible for the housing needs of all their residents. So with private enterprise restricted by building licences and the allocation of materials, local authorities supplied the major part of the million dwellings completed under the direction of the Labour government.[126]

The second task of the construction program was to provide new buildings for the manufacturing industries but this was largely carried out without the intervention of architects. The third requirement was for schools.*

Over five thousand schools had been damaged during the war. The Education Act of 1944, giving the central government the responsibility, through the local educational authorities, of ensuring that all children had facilities for receiving training compatible with their different ages and abilities, made much of the remaining accommodation out of date. Although the number of pupils was less than before the war, an increased birthrate assured a continuing shortage of places in the ensuing sequence of nursery, primary, secondary and further education. Compounding the problem were the population movement into new housing areas and the intended one year raising of the school leaving age which would add a third of a million children to senior classes. To reduce these needs, over seven hundred schools were completed in the next six years.[127]

The government's views on the design of houses and schools were promulgated through circulars and publications such as the Ministry of Health Housing Manuals, originated during the war, and the later Ministry of Education Building Bulletins. These were of a high standard of intelligence and were much admired by the profession. "Unquestionably, the Ministry of Health has taken the lead",[128] wrote the editors of *The Architects' Journal* reviewing the 1949 edition of the Housing Manual.

> Ministry of Education Building Bulletins are setting something of a fashion [they exclaimed on another occasion] . . . they are presented with a rare mixture of logic and imagination which leaves the feeling that many nails are being hit squarely on the head.[129]

Even if local authorities did not share the ministries' opinions, they could not help being influenced by them when housing was subsidized and given low interest loans and grants paid for more than half the cost of education. In these official pronouncements the government let it be known what was expected from architects.

> The architect of today [the Labour party had predicted] is as competent as at any period in our history to design buildings which, while serving their purpose in the most efficient way, are beautiful and reflect the culture, outlook and spirit of the times.[130]

*The buildings and works figures for new housing, manufacturing industries, and education, for 1950 as an example, are in £ millions: 315, 126 and 50, respectively. See Central Statistical Office, *National Income and Expenditure* 1946–1951, London 1952, p. 51.

The test had come.

Wartime introspection had left the progressive British architect more confused than he had been in the nineteen-thirties. At a MARS group public meeting on "What is Modern Architecture?" held at the end of 1944, Mark Hartland Thomas summed up the discussion with the banality that

> Some of you may have come hoping that we who claim to research into this difficult thing would tell you something you did not know before, but the nearest we got to that was when we heard from our friend and brother from the United States [Captain Soontup, that] modern architecture is a combination of functionalism, aesthetics and science.[131]

The post-war resumption of its practice started equally inauspiciously with the first prize in a major competition for a new Crystal Palace cultural and recreational centre being awarded to a neo-Classical design.

> The assessors [stated Kenneth Clark as the assessor representing the Arts Council] have not awarded the prize to a great pioneer work or to a great masterpiece of architecture. A number of pioneer works have been submitted, but they are not workable. The functional buildings look nice but they do not fulfil their functions, while those on *beaux arts* lines do not look quite so nice but are exceedingly functional.[132]

With the example of a brilliantly inventive entry by Clive Entwistle, modern architects got Le Corbusier to voice their protest.

> Will the spirit be betrayed again? [he remonstrated] . . . Architecture is not an ostrich feather stuck with or without grace in a hat by the diligence of a modiste. Architecture is the spirit of truth.[133]

Conditions, however, were against a return to any architectural style based on inbred professionalism. Neither political party was willing to accept architectural mannerisms that interfered with fast, cheap, efficient construction.

> We desire as much as anyone [the coalition Conservative Minister of Works had told the RIBA council a week before the end of the war in Europe] to maintain diversity of design and scope for the individual talents of the architects. But first things must come first. The houses must go up and nothing must stand in their way.[134]

The main bulk of the houses built under the Labour government were without architectural pretensions having neither the conceits of stylistic disciplines nor the popular deceits of the speculator. These buildings were built to function and any additional achievement was gratuitous. Where, as was general, the houses were built of traditional materials, the results were also traditional.

It had been hoped that prefabrication would solve the housing shortage. Aneurin Bevan admitted after a few months as Minister of Health that he had been eagerly looking for a system of mass production that would turn out houses in the same way as cars and aeroplanes, but so far it had eluded him. In the following years, research was carried out by the Ministry of Works, the Ministry of Health, the Building Research Station and other government agencies to discover whether it would be possible to economize in manpower and scarce materials by using new methods of construction. Groups of experimental houses were built and studied in different parts of the country. At the same time the Ministry of Works continued to review proposals submitted by local authorities and private firms and by the final meeting of the special government committee on house construction in 1947, over one hundred alternative prefabricated systems had been approved for development or use.[135] The results were disappointing. With an unconvinced private industry reflecting public preferences, only fifteen percent of the houses built used industrialized methods.

With less of a history of conventional practice or scientific study, apartment buildings permitted a more personal contribution from architects. Initially the qualitative standard was again set by the reactivated firm of Tecton. In Finsbury, London, on a cleared slum site, a four storey serpentine block complemented two eight storey slabs to provide one of the first post-war apartment groupings. While the scale of the divisions of the buildings and their character reflect their low rental origins, the architectural approach is the same as that of their middle class predecessors, Highpoint One and Two. The planning is immaculate and Arup's structure, claimed to be the first reinforced concrete box frame in England, is advanced.* But in the treatment of the slab facades can be seen the dilemma of the functionalist post-war architect with formalistic ambitions. On the one side is a simple brick wall with

*The first box frame structure actually used in Britain appears to be that of Evelyn Court, Hackney, London, a private low rental housing estate. Designed by Burnet, Tait and Lorne, the engineers were D. Bethune-Williams and F. S. Snow. The building was completed in 1935. It employed combined crosswall and floor forms and pumped concrete. The facade infill panels are of brick stuccoed.

windows showing the interior arrangement. On the other side there is a studied composition of balcony balustrades framed into rhythmic proportions that camouflage the orderly tripartite plan behind. The buildings are split between a style applied and a style arising from the reasonable acknowledgment of prevailing conditions. For many modern architects the composed side was unacceptable, being irrational; and the vernacular side was unacceptable, not having the aesthetic prerequisite of looking modern. This dichotomy had to be solved within the stringent realities of the times. While the straightforward approach culminated in St. Pancras Way, London, where the design of a six storey grouping by Norman and Dawbarn relies on the tasteful use of ordinary elements, an acceptable solution was found in the large scale housing development at Churchill Gardens in Westminster, London.[136]

The design was the winning entry of two young graduates, Powell and Moya, in a competition for the housing of over five thousand people. Although the theory of the modern movement was evident in the siting of the tall apartment slabs in parallel lines orientated east and west with low blocks set at right angles between, the buildings at first had brick and window exteriors covering their neat planning and structure. As the plan type changed to reduce costs, however, the use of a box frame structure permitted a more fashionable design with brick and glass articulated in horizontal bands, echoing the Dutch from before the war. The resultant architecture has little intrinsic interest but is of major importance in its successful integration of function with a sufficiently up-to-date expression.

In a more impersonal way, the temporary housing program, although it ended in failure, also upheld the avowed principles of modern architecture. Seemingly an obvious way of getting cheap shelter, one third of the hundred and fifty thousand prefabricated dwellings supplied to local authorities were made of aluminium and constructed in ex-aircraft factories that were mainly government owned. Their final cost was almost double the original estimate and more than that of larger conventional homes.[137] Yet although their economy was spurious and their planning and design were often inferior, their appearance proclaimed their industrial genesis and signified an objective impulse towards a contemporary style. This reached fulfilment in the school building program.

To accommodate the extra pupils resulting from the raising of the school leaving age, the Ministry of Works had offered to supply and erect huts for local authorities under the Hutted Operation for the Raising of the School-leaving Age. Declining to take advantage of these emergency measures, the Hertfordshire County Council asked the Ministry of Education to allow it to develop its own prefabrication system for permanent school building. As in housing, the use of pre-fabrication seemed a logical method of providing a large number of similar units. As early as 1936, G. C. Stillman, County Architect for West Sussex, exploring the feasibility of adaptable structures, had designed and erected experimental classrooms in standardized light steel construction. After the war, the scarcity of traditional materials and craft labour, which where they existed were needed for housing, caused a renewed interest in industrialized methods. This had been anticipated by the wartime committee appointed by the President of the Board of Education to investigate standard construction for schools. Rejecting the advice of school architects, the committee, consisting mainly of educationists and teachers but with Stillman as one of the four architectural representatives, suggested a light steel frame modular structure clad with standardized panel infills.

It is only proper to record here [the committee reported] that representatives of the County Architects' Society . . . expressed doubt how far conditions after the war would be such as to make it either necessary or expedient to abandon the traditional materials and methods of building in favour of any standardisation of planning or use of prefabricated construction. We ourselves take a different view . . .[138]

Limiting itself to statements of principle, the committee suggested further research into the necessary technical detail. The Hertfordshire County Council was permitted to explore these possibilities.

Encouraged by the County Director of Education, an architectural team under Stirrat Johnson-Marshall sought a flexible constructional system that would satisfactorily house school requirements. The architect, as designer and technician, acted as the centre of a group of specialists helping the educationists to formulate problems and collaborating with industrialists in their solution. This empirical approach, assisted by the Building Research Station and regulated by new techniques of cost analysis, produced its first prototype school towards the end of 1946. Within two years a further twenty nine schools had been completed.

The schools produced under these conditions are simple spatial constructions providing serviced volume for the activities of children. Their anonymity is relieved by their modulation of nature. Landscape and light penetrate into the informal classrooms where, unconstrained by any overbearing symbolism, teacher and children can mix in freely changing patterns. The form of each building has no predetermined configuration but derives from the development of the plan within its site. The design proceeds from the components themselves assembled into a visual harmony scaled to the order of the structural module. Idiosyncrasy is proscribed by an authentic pragmatism. The structure is minimal for its function, the surfaces are plain from the factory to be painted with selected colours, the windows are large to give the established daylight requirement. Using the rationale that was their ostensible reason for being, these schools revitalized the stylistic motifs of modern architecture. The resultant aesthetic has a neutrality of logic that was previously eulogized but seldom pursued.

At the same time they cost substantially less than the average school in the rest of the country. In recognition of their success, in 1948 the Ministry of Education set up a new Architects and Building Branch to centralize research and appointed as chief architect Johnson-Marshall who took with him the senior members of the Hertfordshire team. Through government publications their opinions became official policy.

> What is needed [they stated] is a *team* of experts, with the architect responsible for maintaining a balance between all aspects, ensuring that the contribution of each specialist is properly related to the whole . . . This approach to design and building will lead us . . . to new architecture which is a simple and unselfconscious expression of present-day requirements.[139]

The Hertfordshire schools that originated this process epitomized the group practice of architecture. Schools were designed in batches of six and new staff members were permitted to work only upon construction detailing until they had mastered the overall process. Even private architects when they occasionally were commissioned were first required to produce working drawings of a departmental design to familiarize themselves with the prefabricated components. In this way personal temperament was replaced by collective discipline.

The bureaucratic office, with its various divisions where employees find conformity in the slow rise through a graded hierarchy, was the natural organization for this type of approach. The government, representing the people, was its natural client. By 1948 not only did forty percent of practising architects work for government departments but the others received most of their work from government commissions.

It is evident, [stated the report of the RIBA committee to consider the present and future of private architectural practice] that the larger proportion of the public work that has been delegated to private architects is in fact distributed among the bigger or widely known offices . . . Public authorities are understandably anxious to "play safe" in the spending of public monies . . .[140]

The same conditions that could produce the highest common denominator of quality had usually led to the lowest common denominator of mediocrity. Inertia, apathy, indecision: these were the other face of public service; the various levels of local government were widely known for their conventionality. The post-war surge of optimism, however, forced their standards to be raised and gave their staffs the responsibility for responding to the needs of the voters. But while progressive professionals could improve upon the past, they could only proceed as far as public acceptance permitted. For modern architecture to succeed required democratic endorsement. This could be seen clearly in the implementation of the new towns program.

Under an act passed in 1946, although economic difficulties made progress extremely slow, fourteen new towns were started of which eight were scheduled to relieve congestion in the London area. While many adherents of modern architecture worked on their plans and buildings, the overall result is rather a mixture of garden city and suburban practices than a radical implementation of modern architectural theory. The neighbourhoods they created are fashionably tasteful but in an over selfconscious attempt to avoid the errors of the past, the monotony of private enterprise ribbon development is replaced by a loose disorder of variety. The necessarily minimal dwellings look lost along the roadway strips retained from a conventional approach and whereas the neighbourhoods gain homogeneity by having defined edges and communal facilities, with the indecisive treatment of traffic and pedestrians at their centres, they do not solve the social disorganization that was the failure of the pre-war shopping street. Seemingly planning under architects was little better than a free-for-all by speculators. Peterlee was to be the exception.

Approved in response to a request from the local council, this new town in the northern mining area of the county of Durham was to provide housing for a population of thirty thousand and an urban centre for the surrounding villages. The advisory committee under the chairman of the Peterlee Development Corporation decided that if a successful town were to be built, then planning and architecture should be unified by a person who would settle in the area. It was also agreed that all the buildings should be in a coherent modern style. To carry out its intentions the development corporation appointed Lubetkin. Unable to agree with his partners on a suitable working arrangement, the firm of Tecton divided and Lubetkin, at the age of forty-seven, left to continue his career at a magnitude merited by his reputation.

The land for the town contained thirty million tons of coal and in return for the sterilization of part of the site the Ministry of Town and Country Planning had already promised the National Coal Board that only detached and semi-detached houses would be built. Refusing to accept this compromise, Lubetkin designed a compact town spatially defined by highrise apartments. When the National Coal Board denied its technical feasibility, he invited Continental experts to refute its objections. The dispute was referred to the Ministry of Works which while supporting the National Coal Board left the final solution to the disputants. With their continuing failure to agree, the problem was passed to the government. Its decision was to sterilize the land which would have allowed the town to proceed but wasted the coal and deprived the miners of their livelihood. In the consequent renegotiations the chairman of the development corporation changed and the National Coal Board was authorized to establish the pattern of building. Two years had passed and nothing had been built. Lubetkin resigned his last significant commission and virtually withdrew from architectural practice while Peterlee appeared to subside into a conventional community*.[141]

The battle against the disintegration of the town [wrote Richards in *The Architectural Review*] is not a new one. It was one of the great controversial issues of the nineteen-twenties and nineteen-thirties, with the garden-city enthusiasts taking one side and modern architects the other . . . by letting it be imagined that high flats were their sole objective, the town-minded modern architects failed to win a clear cut victory over the garden-suburb sentimentalists . . . And now, when planning theory has been translated into an ambitious post-war building programme, we find that incomplete victory has been turned into total defeat . . . Good design by individual architects does not alter the fact that their failure as a body to give society a lead and

*Initially unable to attract industry, Peterlee grew very slowly with the result that it was able to benefit from changing standards of design. The newer housing is amongst the most pleasant in the country and the town centre is being built as a pedestrian precinct.

impose on it the ideas their knowledge and technical resources tell them are the best ideas, is the failure of modern architecture itself . . .[142]

Architects, then, were not to give the public what it liked but what it was good for it to have. Replying, Brett, the architect-planner of the new town of Hatfield, pointed out that approvals for the design of a new town had to be obtained from the development corporation, the parish council, the district council, a public meeting, the county planning officer, the regional office of the Ministry of Housing and Local Government and planners in the central government. The urbanity that Richards demanded was not wanted and could not be imposed by a professional minority. He might have quoted Richards himself writing in the afterglow of wartime camaraderie.

If democracy means anything, [Richards had written in *The Castles on the Ground*, published in 1946] it means deciding—for a change—to pay some attention to the expressed preference of the majority, to what people themselves want, not what we think they ought to want. We may despise what they want. We may think they should be educated to want something different, or at least to know they could have something different if they wished, instead of their choice being limited by their ignorance of the alternatives; but we can only progress democratically at a speed which does not outpace the slow growth of the public's understanding, in particular its assimilation of social and technical change.[143]

The same was true at the RIBA. Control by government had altered the professional practice of architecture. In pre-war years when Goodhart-Rendel could say in his presidential address that about the only use for government offices was that they gave "regular employment to a number of people that might otherwise have to compete for it in our already crowded market",[144] just over half the members of the RIBA were principals in private practice. By 1948 there had been a sixteen percent decrease of members in private practice and a twenty four percent increase of those in public service.[145]

During the war most architectural students had been conscripted before they could complete their studies and the membership of the RIBA had changed only slowly. In the following years their return, added to an enlarged enrolment, produced a significant increase in the RIBA's numbers. As older architects occupied salaried public appointments, this new influx of graduates became salaried private and public assistants. The result was a decline in the number of principals in an organization that had always assumed that its existence was for their advancement. This new imbalance did not affect control of the RIBA. The difference between employer and employee was initially less marked than between old and young. The rising generation of architects, trained in schools that had discarded the neo-Classical tradition, and maturing within the idealism engendered by the exceptional circumstances of war and reconstruction, equated modernity with progress. By the end of the decade their influence was decisive. Of the ten members elected in 1950 to the RIBA council, seven were known as modern architects and their average age was just over forty.*

While modern architects were capturing the establishment, modern architecture was captivating the public. The process of reconstruction which had provoked the achievement of the Hertfordshire schools mostly produced dull buildings of restricted imagination. Utilitarian means and ends apparently thwarted the talents of the architect. Although government sponsored, the Festival of Britain was to provide the opportunity for him to show what could be done when he was freed to be creative.

Initiated during the war as a suggestion by the Royal Society of Arts to celebrate the centenary of the Great Exhibition of 1851, the idea was later renewed by Gerald Barry, the editor of a London newspaper, and finally changed from an international trade fair into a national cultural exposition. The Festival of Britain was to demonstrate that the country had recovered from the war. Appointed as director-general, Barry brought together an executive committee that included a council for architecture, town planning and building research. The architectural members of this advisory group were all committed to modern architectural theory or practice. Hugh Casson was appointed director of architecture with a small group of coordinating architects and display designers. Seventeen firms were invited to submit designs for specific buildings.

Most of them were under the age of forty [Barry commented afterwards] for we wanted to give as much scope as possible to the younger school to show what they could do.[146]

On May Day 1951, as *The Times* reported, the King and his people went to St. Paul's Cathedral in a joyous mood to declare the Festival of Britain open. Moving on to the South Bank they were greeted by an urban

*Gibberd, Chitty, Stillman, Clarke Hall, Brett, Matthew, and Peter Shepheard.

environment of an elegance and gaiety unknown in contemporary Britain.

Designed in committee, the plan of the site is a masterpiece of picturesque grouping. Deceptively casual, the irregular building forms leave paths that move into a central concourse. Enchantment is gained not with conceptual grandeur but by a myriad of detail that entrances as it changes. Strolling across the fountained plaza, sipping tea above the slowly moving barges of the River Thames, or arguing over the ubiquitous works of art, the visitor found himself in a world worth having fought for.

Yet while its layout was brilliantly instructive, its individual buildings were of an ephemeral mediocrity. Of the pre-war pioneers, Coates and Fry had been given buildings to design on the South Bank, and at Lansbury, the new neighbourhood in east London that was built to coincide with the festival, Frederick Gibberd (an early MARS group member) designed the market centre and Yorke, Rosenberg and Mardall, the nursery and primary schools. Lubetkin had not been invited to participate in the festivities; and Connell had quit Britain after the war to open a practice in east Africa.

The older men failed to maintain the purity of their earlier buildings. Coates decorated the sides of his little cinema with stucco quilting to show that it was theatrical while Fry undulated the roof of his restaurant to indicate lightheartedness. The younger generation was even more involved with trivialities, superimposed over the same indecisiveness that had afflicted progressive British architecture in the nineteen-thirties. The largest building on the South Bank, the Dome of Discovery, was a technical tour de force, a giant aluminium dome hovering over a ring of diagonal steel struts. Destroying the whole idea, massive concrete fins, actually supporting an interior display platform, appeared to take the load of the building and reduced the real structure to a decorative embellishment. Over this omnipresent ambiguity, popular motifs were used to dress up a basic anonymous modernism. Keeping the simple, light, spacious forms of the modern aesthetic, these architects jettisoned the rigid logic of post-war pragmatism. What emerged was not a burst of originality but an ingenuous attempt to give personality to a style now associated with utility. It was successful. The resultant architecture expressed the prevailing public mood for relaxation from a decade of privation. The "contemporary" style became the fashion.

The strength of public reaction can be judged pretty accurately by the comments of the daily press [exulted an editorial in *The Architects'*

Journal entitled 'Modern Architecture Makes Good'], and almost without exception they express approval. Surprise, too, of course, and occasionally mystification, but the really encouraging and delightful fact is that modern architecture, the contemporary style, call it what you will, is overwhelmingly popular.[147]

In contrast, on the adjoining site, the Royal Festival Hall stood aloofly monumental.

Commissioned by the London County Council, the building was the first major work of its rejuvenated architectural department. In 1946, Robert Matthew, who for ten years had been in the Department of Health for Scotland, was appointed the council's chief architect. Two years later Leslie Martin was brought in as his deputy with special responsibility for the design of the concert hall. An early member of the MARS group, Martin had been one of the editors of the pre-war publication on the progressive arts, *Circle*, while head of the school of architecture at Hull. Associated with him for the detailed design of the Royal Festival Hall was another MARS group member Peter Moro.*

The outside of the building recalls the work of Tecton where Moro had worked before the war but, because of its bulk, results in a restless shell rather than an expressive form. The inside is a magnificent exploitation of space that owes more to the ideals of Martin's friend the sculptor Naum Gabo than to any of its British predecessors. Against a background panorama of central London, foyers, galleries, and staircases merge into an ever flowing sequence of varied volumes that takes the visitor into and through the building. At the core, the isolated auditorium shell sits within the circulating levels to be passed under then penetrated to the quietude that is only broken by the balcony clusters surging towards the stage. Too sophisticated and idiosyncratic to be widely approved or influential, the Royal Festival Hall nevertheless set the standard of excellence that was to be reached in the London County Council's future building program.

So the modern architecture that had entered Britain twenty-one years before became the ruling contemporary style. Reaction conceded defeat.

*Moro, who had designed a house at Birdham, Surrey in partnership with Richard Llewelyn Davies before the war, later produced a series of buildings notable for their elegant sophistication. Matthew left the London County Council in 1953 to be professor of architecture at Edinburgh University (and subsequently in private practice with Johnson-Marshall); Martin in 1956 to be professor of architecture at Cambridge University. Llewelyn Davies became professor of architecture at London University in 1960.

During the past quarter of a century [A. E. Richardson, who had been professor of architecture at London University for twenty-seven years, bitterly observed] many experiments have determined the practice of the plastic arts. Fresh tags and labels have explained each innovation . . . Critics urged that the arts and crafts which had accompanied mankind through the centuries were outmoded and ridiculous. It was opined that the time had come when science should take the place of the humbler efforts of the human intellect. The progressive spirit, therefore, has manifested itself in painting, in sculpture, and finally in building. Engineering was looked upon as the rightful successor to architecture, the skeleton of more importance than the form. The incidence of the second world war and the elimination of superfluous human beings presented ideal conditions for progress. Politics led the crusade against heretical backsliding. The results can be looked upon as eminently satisfying to all who have engaged in focusing the particular spirit and genius of the age.[148]

Modern architects had demanded a society that was as modern as their architecture. Comprehensive and rational in their ideals, they had sought a milieu that was planned for their buildings. Their common aims disdained individuality in the ostensible search for communal solutions. The war brought social revolution and with it the fulfilment of their architectural conditions. The MARS group was proved right. Group research directed by a society that accepted planning as a public duty did result in a significant advance in the provision of a new physical environment. The elements of modern architecture, slightly modified, did provide an envelope for the new buildings. The new style did pass from the obsession of a coterie to the expression of a way of life. But by this time the youthful altruism of the elder MARS group members had given way to a worldly self-involvement. The obverse of public patronage was a disinclination for unconforming genius, and hard times restricted even the little personality that had raised some of the architects above the traditionally level standard of Britain. When the community declined Lubetkin's proposals, he retired to the English countryside; Coates returned to Canada to find compensation. The Englishmen, Fry, Yorke and Gibberd successfully evolved an indifferent modernism attuned to the democratic tastes of the community. Only Lucas fulfilled his early ideals by joining the housing division of the London County Council in 1950 after having worked in various government departments. The MARS group lost its reason for being and by CIAM's eighth congress held in Britain in 1951, was disintegrating. But in the same way that the development of public service had coexisted with the elevation of the private modern architect within the profession, so as the public program achieved some success, it was the private modern architect that was welcomed by society.

For the nation's reforming zeal had been halted by an inexorable austerity. The people had looked forward to the fruits of victory; they had been given another five years of rationing. Continuing shortages and recurrent economic crises sapped the good will of the electorate which at the end of its term reduced the government's parliamentary majority to a minimum. Any remaining optimism was dispelled by the effects of the Korean War. Even the government seemed to lose its vitality and in the autumn of 1951 it again dissolved to be defeated at the polls. The people wanted a change. The Festival of Britain symbolized this need, crowding out the memories of the hard days of recovery and heralding a new era of prosperity.

8 NORMALCY

Enthusiasm for a purposeful existence, deadened by the grating realities of life after the war, only slowly reappeared during the nineteen-fifties as pleasure grew in affluence. The Conservative party took over the government in 1951 with a minority of votes but as the decade proceeded the people showed their approval of the evident rise in the standard of living by raising the government majority in successive elections. By 1959, with television, cars and holidays abroad, the increasingly middle class public agreed that it had "never had it so good". The advent of the second post-war Labour government in 1964 with its promises of tough new measures to "get Britain moving" again after a series of debilitating economic and domestic crises, did little to alter the general pattern of prosperity at home and insolvency abroad. And although its *National Plan*, published in 1965 (and soon outdated when yet another financial crisis forced the devaluation of the pound), promised orderly constructional growth, the stop-go methods of the Conservative government were simply bureaucratized when the licensing of major private buildings was reimposed in 1966.

The concurrent expansion of building activity, doubling over the Conservative government's span in office through a series of booms and lulls, initially brought little of architectural interest. While the Festival of Britain had heartened modern architects, its fashions were more easily exploited through the consumer tastes of young home furnishers than in the commissioning and designing of buildings dominated by the older generation. With the length of the war and architectural education, and the difficulties of setting up in independent practice, nearly three-quarters of all principal architects were over forty years of age and most of these had been trained in offices involved in everyday practicalities and not in the more aesthetically conscious schools.[149] Their level of attainment was generally outmoded and mediocre producing non-descript arrangements faced in masonry carrying neo-Georgian stylistic overtones.

Private practitioners of modern architecture were little more incisive. Their cubic forms delineated by the structural grid, faced with glass and panel (rather than the continuous surface of prewar years), and balanced by occasional solid walling, housed rectangular rooms of simple disposition opened up where suitable into larger spaces. Although visually and technically more up to date, most of these buildings are neither necessarily more satisfying nor more practicable or economic than their conservative counterparts. They lack a specific motivating intent, aesthetic or functional, emotional or intellectual, particular or general, and rely for their effect on a commonplace usage of architectural motifs which, to their admirers, carried the paramount virtue of relevance to the Zeitgeist regardless of the purpose to which they were put.

The style at its best, similar in its general appearance but refined into an architectural expression, is seen in the work of Powell and Moya. Their varied practice including housing, hospitals, schools and university buildings, maintained a consistently high standard of design exemplified in the Mayfield School, Putney, London completed in 1955. The success of this building lies in its elegant simplicity of proportion and material, its spatial ease and fullness, and the charm of its features.

But even the buildings of Powell and Moya do not have the symbolic intensity generally required by connoisseurs of works of art. Nor did they extend the experienced range of architectural effects. The modern architect, familiar with the canons of the International Style, could reach the fullness of known awareness and did not wish for anything further. The younger generation, seeking inspiration and initially denied the attraction of Le Corbusier whose last significant buildings had been completed in the nineteen-thirties, demanded more evidence of genius. With the publication in the nineteen-forties of Mies van der Rohe's designs for the Illinois Institute of Technology campus, another architectural discipline was made available, seemingly more attuned to the postwar involvement with frame and infill. Modern architecture by becoming respectable had subverted the avant-garde; in 1950, the Smithsons, brilliantly adapting the Miesian aesthetic in their winning competition design for a school in Hunstanton, Norfolk, appeared to reestablish it.

Educated at the University of Durham, Alison and Peter Smithson had married in 1949 and worked in the schools division of the London County Council architectural department. Their plan, however, had nothing in common with the extended pavilion arrangement previously favoured by most specialists including the competition assessor Clarke Hall whose prewar News Chronicle design had been reduced, adapted and built at Richmond, Yorkshire in 1940. With its classrooms grouped around two courts and raised around and above the hall and service rooms below, the Smithsons' building was unequivocally formal in its composition. Its impact was lessened by the postponement of its construction but meanwhile the Smithsons advanced their position as leaders of the avant-garde with two unplaced competition entries for Coventry cathedral and housing at Golden Lane, London. While the first of these projects was purely a simplistic form of sophisticated engineering, the second was of seminal importance for British architects in introducing the idea of apartment slab access decks based on Le Corbusier's Îlot Insalubre designs published in his *Oeuvre Complète* in 1939. For not only were the Smithsons talented designers; they were also messianic in their practice. In 1953 the influence of their pronouncements was greatly extended when two of their admirers, Theo Crosby and Reyner Banham, joined the editorial staffs of *Architectural Design* and *The Architectural Review*.

> Now that the New Brutalism has found a home in your pages [wrote a correspondent to *The Architectural Review*], perhaps your readers would be interested to hear of the reaction of AA students. As one of the initiators of the AA Forum on 'Parallels of Life and Art' at which both Peter Smithson and Basil Taylor were speakers, I was particularly interested to see that student feeling was running very strongly against the exhibition—the aesthetic source of the New Brutalism. It was variously condemned as shallow, eclectic, an example of the New Picturesque and denying the spiritual in man. As a result of this discussion one of your editorial colleagues at a recent seminar at the Institute of Contemporary Art labelled the AA students as a reactionary body![150]

The Hunstanton school was not completed until 1954 by which time the Smithsons had modified their point of departure, later characteristically summarizing their reasons for this as "MIES IS GREAT BUT CORB COMMUNICATES".[151] Le Corbusier's Unité d'Habitation at Marseilles with its majestic geometry in rough concrete, which although not completed until 1952 had been building since 1948 and whose presence was there to experience, became the focus of the younger generation's adulation and inspiration. The new credo, demanding a directness of means and effect, provoked agitated responses from the orthodox modern architect. "Who is pulling whose leg?"[152] enquired Richard Llewelyn Davies and John Weeks; "a pretended new movement jocularly designated"[153] commented John Summerson.

Due to the unorthodoxies of the plan and of the details [*The Architects'*
Journal editorialized on the completed Hunstanton school], this
building is likely to attract a great deal of attention as an example of
"modern architecture". It cannot, however, fairly be said to deserve
the full implications of the title. . . . Indeed, in that this building
seems often to ignore the children for which it is built, it is hard to
define it as *architecture* at all. It is a formalist structure which will
please only the architects, and a small coterie concerned more with
satisfying their personal design sense than with achieving a humanist,
functional, architecture.[154]

The Hunstanton school is functionally inadequate, technically naive,
noisy, cold and dirty. It contributed nothing to the evolution of school
building design and is expensive to maintain. Visually its acme was
reached when it was photographed on completion without furniture
or children at the architects' request. Yet its elemental image and
ostensibly robust honesty gratified the everpresent hope in many
architects that the developing complexity and, presumed, consequent
devitalization of architecture could be turned aside by purity much in
the same way that the simple-minded were once believed to possess
supernatural powers.

While the Hunstanton school clearly expressed an architectural
attitude, the Smithsons in their written statements preferred assertive
encyclicals to reasoned argument. Their terminology was simple but
obscure, many of their meanings seeming to have been expounded
elsewhere although their desired consequences were obviously different.
But if the originality or usefulness of their ideas were questionable, their
insistence on an operational ethic endowed the profession with an
architectural conscience.

The schools and institutes [proclaimed Peter Smithson in a discussion
on futurism and modern architecture] should attempt to focus their
students with the same energy on the plastic systems . . . as they do on
technique. Now we may say such a statement in favour of academies
conflicts with my personal opinions, which have been all my life long
directed against academic architecture. But it is impossible to construct a meaningful dynamic between a new system and a muddle.
If people were aware of what they were doing and why they were
doing it, it might be possible for them to comprehend the antithesis,
the new system.[155]

The Smithsons' admittance into the MARS group in 1953 confronted an
establishment of modern architects who since the war had not only seen

their ideals widely assimilated by government and society but had also become older and influential and were therefore able to utilize more conventional national and international institutions for the furtherance of their aims. When the organization of the parent body CIAM was handed over to a committee of younger members including the Smithsons, their reformulation of an avant-garde movement rejecting previous and other dogmas led to its disintegration and the subsequent disbandment of the MARS group at the beginning of 1957.[156]*

While the evident purposefulness of the Smithsons excited a following, their published projects continued to show little stylistic continuity and their second building of any consequence, for *The Economist*, London was not completed until ten years after their first. In the meantime, even if the Smithsons were, as Banham phrased it, "not offering a style but a set of moral responsibilities",[157] their stimulated progeny were seeking a set of forms.

The transference of the postwar Corbusian image across the English Channel was achieved by the newly formed housing division of the London County Council architectural department. Responsibility for the design of housing, previously placed with the valuer's department, had been handed over to the architectural department at the beginning of 1950 and placed under the leadership of Whitfield Lewis. As increasingly occurred with other enlightened architectural departments, the large staff, which in the housing division soon included around 300 architects with an annual building program of £20 million, was divided into relatively autonomous groups, teamwork replacing the traditional office structure of pyramidical responsibility. The first housing project to be designed in the new division was the Ackroydon Estate, Wimbledon, an arrangement of 11-storey towers and lower terraces which set the pattern for future mixed developments. This and the contemporaneous Alton East Estate at Roehampton had a somewhat Scandinavian flavour favoured by Lewis and reminiscent of current Swedish housing; the next significant project, the Alton West Estate, Roehampton bore the imprint of Marseilles. Under the supervision of Lucas, a team of recent graduates reinterpreted the Ville Radieuse. The stylistic base moved from those who thought the Unité d'Habitation too arbitrary, too abstract and too monumental ("it is interesting that in Moscow Corbusier is accused of Fascist tendencies"), to those who found there "a whole structure, a whole set of components, a whole series of spaces, designed on a system of dimensions all harmonically related".[158]

*For the flavour of their critical approach to others, see Oscar Newman, CIAM '59 *in Otterlo*, Hilversum 1961.

Designed 1952–3 and built 1955–9, the Alton West Estate is located in and between parkland, housing a population of over six and a half thousand with schools, shops and other community facilities. Two clusters of 12-storey point blocks and a series of five 10-storey slabs, raised on columns stepping down a grass slope, articulate the site of one hundred acres creating an environment of urban living in country landscape that had long been the ideal of modern architects. Sufficiently robust to prevail over the mundane organization of traffic below, the tall buildings are elegantly detailed, their poured and precast reinforced concrete structures being faced with a precast concrete cladding which unifies the two dwelling types, the one utilizing a maisonette section, the other continuing the grouped apartment plan of the earlier tower designs.

Unfortunately the conceptual unity of the tall buildings does not extend to the rows of 4-storey maisonettes or houses, perhaps because Le Corbusier had largely ignored the problem of small scale repetitive dwellings. These lower units with their brick crosswall construction and wood and glass infill not only differ in character to the tall blocks but their urban terrace form, used apart from its structuring system of streets, both lacks containment to length and height, and is rigid and disjointed in its new landscape setting.

These problems of form and character were solved by Stirling and Gowan, once again assisted by Le Corbusier whose Jaoul houses under construction had been intimately studied. The first commission of two youthful partners who had previously worked together in the firm of Lyons, Israel and Ellis, the apartment buildings at Ham Common, completed in 1958, introduced a new vernacular of concrete and brick, the contemporary material exaggerating the structural organization of the form while the traditional material provides a domestic scale and texture; for although in fact the external brickwork is load bearing in the 3-storey block, it is indented to complement the wood-framed windows and appears structurally subordinate to the horizontal slabs. The building form, also indented, is freed from a rigid street-front composition and angles down its garden strip site to model its locality.

The spread of a reinforced concrete style was advanced by the changing economics of multistorey construction. Although steel manufacturers were initially reluctant to transfer production from heavy sections to reinforcements, consumption of the latter increased disproportionately as by the mid nineteen-fifties it became cheaper to build in reinforced concrete than steel.[159] The rise in the cost of site labour encouraged prefabrication and mechanization and within a few years hundreds of tower cranes followed the original importations from the Continent first used in Britain commercially at the beginning of 1951 and almost simultaneously tested by the Building Research Station.* Their profitable use required the rationalization of the building process bringing to traditionally casual construction sites the disciplines of assembly production.

While the constructional method of the Alton West Estate was the normal particular solution to a specific problem, the London County Council used the Elmington Estate, Camberwell, built 1955–7, to investigate the complexities of systematic design. A team representing architects, surveyors, engineers, the Building Research Station and the contractor, who had been invited to join the team before detailed designing was begun, compared the suitability and cost of alternative constructional elements. The use of a tower crane permitted the extensive prefabrication of parts set into a poured structure of alternating reinforced and unreinforced crosswalls.

Thus the housing division of the London County Council with its design and technological competence joined the Hertfordshire schools division as official pacemakers. But while its landscaped balanced residential areas were the enlightened ideal, a new urban image was arising in Sheffield.

The Smithsons' use of wide access decks in the Golden Lane housing competition had been paralleled in the entry of Jack Lynn and Gordon Ryder, their classmates from Newcastle, and also in an AA housing thesis by Ivor Smith who was acquainted with both the Smithsons and Lynn. The subsequent collaboration by Smith and Lynn on a further housing study took them to the recently appointed city architect at Sheffield, J. L. Womersley, who invited them to collaborate on the Park Hill redevelopment area. Designed 1953–5 and built 1957–61, the structural engineers were once again the firm of Arup and the quantity surveyors, that of Sweett.

Housing 3,500 at a density of nearly 200 persons per acre, its serpentine interconnected blocks range over a steeply sloping site overlooking the city centre in the valley. With the consequent heights varying from four to fourteen storeys, ten feet wide decks serve three floors of accommodation, entering maisonettes directly and apartments below, each except the top deck meeting the ground at its upper level. The frame

---

*The first tower crane appears to have been imported from France and used by the firm of John Laing in the erection of apartment buildings for the Fulham Borough Council early in 1951. The BRS crane was imported from Germany. See "A new type of crane", *The Builder*, CLXXX, 1951, p. 564.

structure, filled with brick panels of varying colour, is of reinforced concrete stiffened by the staircase enclosures. At strategic points, pubs and other community amenities are set into the buildings which circumscribe a primary school, shops and playgrounds.

The wall of residences modelling the hillside creates an original urban image suggested by Le Corbusier in his Algiers project but never previously built in Britain. Its phalanx dominates the city centre below; at night it provides a sparkling backdrop. The stacked decks inventively discard the concept of the multiple dwelling block as an over-enlarged house and conclusively illustrate the potential organizational freedom of elevated walkways. Unfortunately, as built, they are also ugly and ill-shaped with doorways stunted in scale, and quasi-doorsteps. Swept with wind and echoing with noise, they have an even meaner character than the East End slums of London whose street life was much admired by the Smithsons and some of their associates. Overreacting to a supposed prissiness associated with the architecture of the older generation, the architects have consciously sought a tough aesthetic that has simply degenerated into squalor.*

Our predecessors [wrote the committee under the chairmanship of Sir Parker Morris in its 1961 report on housing standards] . . . were necessarily working against the background of the 'thirties, now nearly a quarter of a century away, with vastly different problems, outlook and trends. Since the end of the war, the country has undergone a social and economic revolution, and the pattern of living is still changing fast. There is full employment, a national health service, and the various social insurance benefits such as family allowances and retirement pensions. In material terms people are better off than ever before; the average pay packet nowadays buys a good deal more than it did in 1939, and to this four million working wives and the teenagers add their own contribution. One household in three has a car; the same proportion have a washing machine. Television sets are owned by two households in three; so are vacuum cleaners; and one household in five has a refrigerator. These possessions are spreading fast through all income groups, fastest of all in the lowest brackets, and we are promised a doubled standard of living in 25

---

*The difference between the generations can be seen on London's South Bank where the new arts complex completed in 1968 conflicts with the Royal Festival Hall, seventeen years its senior. The ambivalent reaction to sophistication amongst some younger architects may be observed in the contrast between the intricacy of method used to make the concrete look like wood treated to look like concrete and the aridity of its effect.

years . . . the times demand change and improvement in our new housing . . . The country already possesses a large stock of houses and flats that are becoming out-of-date and cannot afford to go on building more of them. Better homes will cost more money; but we are sure that a sufficient number of people . . . are prepared to pay the extra charges for the better article."[160]*

It is difficult to separate the social and aesthetic characteristics of housing as its architectural character derives both from economic and real or imaginary sociological limitations, and also from the form that the architect gives to his solution. Nevertheless it is evident that although postwar local authority housing was greatly superior to the housing it replaced particularly in the design of its individual dwelling units, the environmental standards of its communal spaces and approaches, especially in apartment projects, often remained far below that generally acceptable to middle-class tenants. That this is due to some extent to the architect's ideology can be seen at the Roehampton estates, the "Swedish" buildings providing a standard milieu, the "Corbusian" buildings initiating the move towards a rougher gregariousness supposedly more in character with working-class habits.

The main recommendations of the Parker Morris report called for better heating and more internal space arranged so that its occupants could live as they wished; outside proposals included better children's playspaces and the absorption of cars. The report was emphatic on the need to employ architects especially in the overall design of the environment and rebuked "private developers who remain wedded to old plans grown dusty with the years",[161] recognizing the lack of quality in much of their work which under the Conservative government reached over sixty percent of all new housing in the early nineteen-sixties.

A notable exception to the pitch-roofed bay-windowed detached bungalows or houses on separate plots fronting access roads conventionally favoured by home purchasers and building societies, was the work of Span. Mostly located in London suburbs, designed by Eric Lyons and built by an ex-architectural partner G. P. Townsend who resigned from the RIBA in 1954 to act as developer, the simple materials used

---

*Contrary to the Parker Morris report, increasing affluence expressed itself not so much in demands for higher environmental standards as in more cars. An interesting example is the mid-nineteenth century model town of Saltaire, Yorkshire whose houses, now mainly individually owned, are neatly painted and furnished by proud inhabitants who seem unconcerned by outside toilets and the lack of baths and other amenities.

by this company form boxy terraces often enclosing courts in richly planted estates.

While the Parker Morris standards were not yet mandatory, by 1968 over half of the new local authority dwellings incorporated all the recommended improvements. An excellent example of these higher standards is the St. Mary's Estate, Oldham, Lancashire, a sixteen acre slum clearance program completed in 1967. Housing 110 persons per acre, terraces sited along a ridge are flanked by low blocks set into the slopes and served by Park Hill type continuous access decks raised around landscaped squares. Designed in the Ministry of Housing (in collaboration with Max Lock and the borough architect), the project further exemplifies the advance of development groups and building industrialization.

In November 1954 the government ended the restraints on private building that had been in existence for fifteen years.*

[This issue, wrote the editors of *The Architectural Review* celebrating the event] can be regarded as the last of the prison-cell issues. As such, it reveals a great deal of vitality behind bars. Architecture is eagerly shaking itself free of the restrictions that have shackled it for so long, and next year it should be possible to employ a survey like this as a test of what the contemporary architect can do instead of, as hitherto, a record of the limitations within which he has to work.[162]

Nearly four years later, the only British illustration to an article inveighing against the widespread intemperance of modern architects was a secluded carpet factory weaving shed in Wiltshire.[163] In contrast to the virtuosity of the younger generation of Americans, personal inventiveness was a rare British attribute. When forms more complex than those based on rectangles began to be used, the results were usually bizarre. An early example, Trinity School, Southwark, London designed by Chamberlin, Powell and Bon and completed in 1960, links a pentagonal assembly hall block covered by five hyperbolic sections to a catenary roofed gymnasium. Subsequently another hyperbolic paraboloidal structure, equally inapposite, was incorporated into London's Commonwealth Institute.

The first original talent to appear was that of Denys Lasdun, a Tecton partner at the time of its dissolution. Born in 1914, Lasdun

---

*This had little effect on the total amount of new construction over the next few years as the boom which resulted in the official removal of building licensing was followed by a four year lull. It did however have a psychological impact on architects who could then set aside asceticism with an easy conscience.

spanned the significant gap between those who initiated the modern movement in Britain and those who came into it after the war. A pre-war employee (and associate) of Coates and later Tecton, he was also chairman of the MARS group working team which included the Smithsons and their contemporaries. Close to a house he had designed seventeen years earlier, his first building of consequence was the primary school completed in 1955 within the Hallfield Estate, Paddington, London which was initially a Tecton project under his direction before being taken over by the new partnership of Drake and Lasdun as part of their dissolution settlement.

Its 2-storey sinuous block contains junior classrooms along half its length, the other half vertically interlocking infant and junior administrative areas with assembly halls in an arcuated form linked through to a grouping of polygonal infant classrooms. A potent hieroglyph when seen bird's-eye from surrounding highrise apartment slabs, at ground level the building abounds in sensuous details from the play of light and shade on modelled louvres along an upper corridor to the hexagonal peephole in the infants' microworld.

Lasdun's interest at that time in current sociological analogues led to two projects of so-called 'cluster blocks' in Bethnal Green, London designed from 1953 onwards with a 14-storey unit being completed in 1959.* Four shafts of 2-bedroom semi-detached maisonettes are linked by short bridges to a vertical service core, supposedly providing privacy and maintaining household identity and at the same time increasing density and creating a neighbourhood focus. While its sociological achievements remain unproven and the form was never further developed presumably being too disjointed for what it accomplishes, the design marks a break between a stylistic vocabulary derived from Tecton and the simple melodic elegance of Lasdun's later buildings.

Like Tecton's buildings, the school and cluster blocks, although deriving from a different conceptual basis, are pictorial in their composition being more evocative in plan and elevation than in their disposition of forms. Lacking a compensating three-dimensional visual order, their surface patterns inexorably lose their attractiveness as uneven weather-

*It has been inferred that Lasdun was inspired by Kevin Lynch's article on "The form of cities", (*Scientific American*, CXC (No. 4), 1954, pp. 54–63), in which Lynch argued that the functional differentiation of urban components (grain) should be neither too fine nor too coarse but derived from optimum clusters. The "cluster blocks" at Usk Street, however, were designed before the article—in 1953. The Smithsons, whose pictorial article on "Cluster patterns", (*Architecture and Building*, XXXI, 1956, pp. 271–272), more closely follows Lynch's ideas, claim to have designed their first "cluster city" in 1952.

ing, often combined with poor maintenance, breaks up their purity of line, shape and colour.

In the luxury apartment building facing Green Park, London also completed in 1960, with its cleverly inflated scale produced by the sectional device of interlocking and accentuating differing living room heights, and its expensive materials of engineering brick, granite, mosaic and bronze, these shortcomings no longer exist.

Similarly in the equally prestigious building for the Royal College of Physicians in Regent's Park, London, enduring materials (except for the exposed concrete in the so-called "service" elements) create a form of exterior and interior fascination. Typically many years in its realization evidencing the care shown in the design, the building was commissioned in 1959 and completed in 1964. Its main fashionable inverted ziggurat form is achieved by cantilevering a third floor gallery around its double storey library and placing a pair of columns about its glazed entrance doorways. This rectangularity is softened by roof and base elements, both visually successful yet intellectually irritating. Deceptively funnel-like shafts mount the roof shaping only the facade of elevator towers; and alongside the main building, a novel warped form sits around and over what is inside a sunken, conventionally modern auditorium. Nonetheless the building regally invades the park from a backdrop of terrace infill office space fronting the bordering street, while the south side opens up with visceral mystery as it spills out from around the sanctum of the censor's office onto the terraces of the members' rooms and, inside, unwinds upwards through the central staircase volume which connects the main front and rear plan components of library and dining hall. If its parts often substitute rationalizations for reason, the building as a whole is a persuasive work of art.

Conditioned to austerity and cooperation, British architects were ambivalent towards architecture as art. The RIBA insisted on the systemization of professional skills yet invited Louis Kahn to give its annual discourse in 1962 and then called in the police to control the crowds that were turned away. *The Architectural Review* even blamed the loss of senior talent from public to private practice, in the shift that occurred after the peak of official employment in the mid nineteen-fifties, on the seduction of personal expression rather than on the ordinary benefits of independence.

It is an interesting fact [wrote its editors in 1965] that the change from the enthusiasm for the public office to preference for the private office has coincided with the change from the anonymous, inter-

national, largely rectilinear style of architecture to a more individualistic and sculptural style. Is this significant? . . . Public authority
architecture does least to cater for the vanity that is said to be many
artists' driving-force, but it would be a strange thing, demanding a
cynical assessment of the present-day architect's view of his job, if the
cause of his declining interest in the town hall was to turn out to be
simply his vanity.[164]

The opportunity for experimentation by a younger generation of
architects, commonly school trained and sophisticated by the world-
wide dissemination of a modern architectural idiom, was considerably
increased with the upsurge in university building which, slow to remedy
the low national percentage of higher education in the nineteen-fifties,
quickened in the nineteen-sixties in response to the demands of the
postwar bulge in population. In 1959 the government authorized the
new University of Sussex designed by Basil Spence; in the following
year those of York by Matthew, Johnson-Marshall and East Anglia at
Norwich by Lasdun. But the breakthrough in architectural style had
occurred earlier in the atrophied environment of Cambridge with the
Arts Faculties design by Casson and Conder chosen in a limited
competition in 1953. Eclectic yet urbane, these buildings completed
from 1959 on presaged many notable designs including the University
Club House by the established Architects' Co-Partnership,* its shed-
like forms spilling down the steep river bank at Durham, and the
robust brick and concrete residential block for the Theological College at
Chichester by the youthful partnership of Ahrends, Burton and
Koralek. The preeminent university building, however, was the
Engineering Building at Leicester University designed by Stirling and
Gowan and completed in 1963.

Recipient of the 1965 R. S. Reynolds Memorial Award and selected
by leading architects immediately after its opening as one of the two
most interesting British buildings of the preceding decade (the other
being the Alton West Estate), the Engineering building attracted wide
critical acclaim.[165]

Feeling and knowing as we have for the past two generations, [wrote
the American historian John Jacobus] how is it possible that this

*The firm, then known as the Architects Co-operative Partnership, was
responsible for one of the first large post-war buildings in the modern style—the
rubber factory at Brynmawr in Wales, designed through 1945 and completed in
1951. One of the partners, Leo de Syllas (1917–1964) had been the editor of
Focus.

193

N

achievement is the exception and not the rule? Isn't the functional clarity which this building documents the very thing which, we have been told, contemporary architecture is all about? Of course, in many respects we have allowed ourselves to be misled, especially about the architecture of the 'twenties, almost invariably more cubist than practical . . .[166]

Although the practicalities of the Engineering Building include oddities such as its entrance ramp and spiral stair, the individually formed and profiled parts of its tower impart a character of rectitude and lucidity. The juxtaposed higher and lower office and laboratory towers are set over smaller and larger lecture theatres at differing levels and are connected to an ordering vertical core by planes of glass that open up glazed views as the building is ascended. With its angled clerestory lighting, chamfered edges (ostensibly due to building lines) and other enrichments of form unified by red tile and engineering brick and aluminium patent glazing, the Engineering Building alleviated functionalism with sensibility to become one of Britain's foremost architectural images.*

Through each successive post-Festival of Britain year, the enlightened architectural press announced the long awaited victory of the modern style. However, only school buildings continued to provide a consistently modern building type. "How did you", asked the Minister of Education on the occasion of opening Hertfordshire's one hundredth postwar school at the beginning of 1955, "contrive to be both businesslike and beautiful".[167] The success of the school building program came with its ease of collaboration between the central government and relatively few large educational authorities, and its sheltering by both political parties from the periodic financial cuts that confounded long

*The partnership of Stirling and Gowan terminated in 1963. Stirling's History Faculty building for Cambridge University, situated near Casson and Conder's arts buildings and Martin and Wilson's fine Aalto-like Caius residences, was completed in 1968. Probably the most inventive building in Britain with a superb interior space, the History Faculty building appears, like the Engineering building, to have had glazing problems (the Engineering building was leaking profusely when visited in September 1968), and to be mechanically difficult. The incongruous effects of stretching functionalism to gain an architectural experience may likewise be seen in Lasdun's University of East Anglia still under construction (1968) where exciting residential terraces back up a non-existent hill to unpleasant walkways elevated over a delightful grassy slope. "*Pourquoi cette séparation?*" asks Lasdun rhetorically in an article in *l'Architecture d'Aujourd' hui* (No. 139, 1968, p. 40). "Non pas à cause des accidents, mais *parce que tout moment consacré à la marche est un moment de réflexion.*"

term arrangements in other local government departments.[168] With the appointment of Donald Gibson as county architect to Nottinghamshire after his departure from Coventry in 1955, another series of events continued its rationalization.

The Ministry of Education had been experimenting in its development program with various structural methods as well as encouraging the industry to develop alternate systems. When the Nottinghamshire county architects, who had been joined by Dan Lacey and Henry Swain from Hertfordshire, investigated the various systems available which might be modified to solve the problem of building economically over ground subject to mining subsidence, they chose the pin-jointed cold rolled structural frame based on a forty inch grid, previously used by the Ministry of Education at Belper, Derbyshire. After examining the performance of recently completed schools with the county educationists, the architectural team then analysed each constructional element to determine its particular needs and, in collaboration with manufacturers, designed a set of standard components. The first school built in the new system was started at the beginning of 1957. Later that year the Ministry of Education brought together other interested school building authorities, six of whom with Nottinghamshire formed CLASP, the Consortium of Local Authorities Special Programme.[169]

The consortium was directed by its chief architects meeting quarterly supplemented by monthly working parties of representative architects and quantity surveyors. While each member was responsible for its own building program, the work of research and development was financed by the allocation of one quarter percent of its cost and shared. This annual value, initially largely representing Nottinghamshire's total school building budget, decupled in the first six years and by 1963 had reached £10 million. The resultant possibility of bulk purchasing and serial contracting reduced the cost of CLASP schools below the national average and permitted their increased quality. Detailed in over one hundred standard drawings, CLASP became the first prefabricated component system to be sponsored and controlled by architects and consumers who through competitive tendering were able to acquire the economic benefits of quantity production.

Although the CLASP system was usually multistorey, being mainly used for secondary schools rather than the primary schools of the earlier Hertfordshire program, its simple flat-topped cubic forms clad with wood windows and concrete, clay, wood or aluminium units, have the same informal attractiveness as their predecessors. At their most lavish and elegant as in the John F. Kennedy School, Coventry, completed in 1967, the buildings create a humane, polished, expansive educational environment.*

On an even larger scale, the CLASP system was used by Matthew, Johnson-Marshall in their designs for York University. Selected to enable the buildings to be erected for early occupancy, the industrialized process employed in the simple serrated blocks of the residential colleges is enlivened by the special forms of major focal buildings and mellowed by the superb landscape and its charming details as where stepping stones pass through the artificial lake under the raked underside of a major lecture hall.

And so as this successful use of the CLASP system in Britain proceeded through the nineteen-sixties, its international reputation was also established at the 1960 Milan Triennale where a typical school designed in Nottinghamshire for the display theme of "Home and School" was awarded a *gran premio con menzione speciale*.

The achievements of CLASP, deriving both from its association of local authorities and the stimulus of its development group, soon encouraged other formations. Elaborated in the Ministry of Education which used experimental projects to test new ways of building economically and well while clarifying for the architect the needs of his client, development groups later proliferated in other government departments. Similarly other consortia were also organized, from 1962 on largely concentrating on housing in response to a shift in government priorities. While some of these concerned themselves with rationalizing traditional construction, a renewed interest arose in industrialization.

Once considered a panacea for postwar reconstruction, the use of industrialized processes had reached its low peak in the early nineteen-fifties and declined with the rise of private building. System sponsors, in an industry with a multiplicity of clients serviced by diverse small professional groups utilizing open tendering amongst innumerable contractors, found no consistent markets and no way to impose the use of a standardized production. However, an expanding building program with a static labour force in which traditional skills were increasingly rare, encouraged an improvement in productivity. With substantial mechanization, individual output was brought back to its pre-war level.

---

*An interesting situation has arisen where Nottinghamshire, the county that pioneered the CLASP system and speeded the construction of its schools, now finds itself eleven years later with an inappropriate assortment of separate grammar and secondary modern school buildings unsuited to the Labour government's policy of combined comprehensive education.

It is curious [observed Peter Trench, Director of the National Federation of Building Trade Employers, in 1960] that we have only recently arrived at a stage where the cost of site labour has made large-scale mechanisation an economic proposition, not only because it has led to a reduction in overall costs, but because the whole building process has been speeded up . . .[170]

Large building contractors, requiring effectual and continuous employment of expensive plant, either imported industrialized systems from more advanced Continental countries or developed their own. Similarly manufacturers seeking new markets for their building materials incorporated them into prefabricated parts to be assembled by their own operatives or in association with selected contractors. Meanwhile the government itself, with forty percent of all new construction publicly commissioned, was also considering proposals for reducing time and costs.

The Government [reported Sir Harold Emmerson to the Minister of Works in his *Survey of Problems before the Construction Industries* published in 1962] has an interest in increased efficiency, partly as representing the building owner in the public sector, and partly because of its responsibility for promoting economic growth for the country as a whole. This calls for a new form of relationship between Government and the construction industries.[171]

At the end of 1963 the formation of a National Building Agency was announced for promoting further consortia by extending to public authorities and private clients the advantages of shared experience and bulk buying facilities. While initially placed with the Ministry of Public Building and Works, the Labour government with its traditional stress on housing output transferred the National Building Agency to the Ministry of Housing where it concentrated on appraising housing systems for public and private builders and providing professional advice on their use in coordinated programs. In little more than a year after its organization under its chief architect Barr (who after the war had worked at Hertfordshire, London County Council and the Ministry of Education before becoming the chief architect at the Ministry of Housing), it had shortlisted over a hundred house building systems. By 1966, over one-third of public housing was utilizing industrialized construction.[172]

At the same time the Ministry of Housing was also experimenting with its own low-rise and medium-rise designs, the latter being the 12M (M representing a 4in./10cm module) used in the St. Mary's Estate, Oldham which was evolved in collaboration with the engineers Arup and

197

the firm of John Laing who manufactured the concrete panels under licence from the Jespersen Organization of Denmark. Concurrent with this coordination of housing activity, the consolidation of government research and development under Gibson by the Conservative government in 1962 was extended under the Labour government in 1967 to include all departmental building with an annual program of over £250 million carried out by a professional staff of over two thousand.

This process of rationalization in the building industry and government was paralleled in the architectural profession. The RIBA membership, growing rapidly during the nineteen-fifties as the percentage of registered architects who joined it burgeoned, reached a United Kingdom total of 14,000 by the middle of the decade. Its constitution, however, continued to be haphazard and autocratic, based on a loose relationship between the central body and local Allied Societies outside and extra to the RIBA whose composition and character had been individually determined by historical evolution. Their independence manifested itself in their variety of methods for appointing one third of the members of the RIBA council so that even the RIBA was unable to tell how far these arrived through democratic procedures.[173]

Composed of over seventy persons, only thirty members of the RIBA council were elected by national balloting. Although a voting pattern was never discerned, one of the paths to success as a national candidate was evidently professional fame: the membership was ill-prepared to vote upon any other basis.* Closed council meetings and the reluctance of many candidates to expose their views even when prodded by *The Architects' Journal* gave voters little opportunity to hear candidates' aims or observe their diplomatic skills. The national list, heavily weighted towards the senior fellowship category, naturally drew its familiar names from principals in private and public practice while a majority of electors were salaried assistants. The placing of power in the RIBA council encouraged paternal conservatism by permitting outside access to important positions through special appointments to its executive committee. As for its chief adviser, C. D. Spragg had become RIBA secretary on MacAlister's retirement after being his assistant for nineteen years, and had worked at the RIBA since before the First World War.†

*Buchanan's report on *Traffic in Towns* was published in 1963. The following year he stood for election to the RIBA council and received 4675 votes, 987 more than Lyons and 1705 more than Johnson-Marshall who came third on the list.

†Everard Haynes was secretary of the influential Board of Architectural Education for forty-two years, 1921–1963.

In 1955 the membership rebelled. Frustrated by the establishment's view of its image as a learned society which could apparently concern itself with fees but not with salaries, the first floor motion for forty years was placed before the annual general meeting and the RIBA council was censured. The leadership moved, but too slowly. A committee chaired by Richard Sheppard, set up to investigate the structure of the profession and how its members in salaried employment could be more satisfactorily represented, received the help of a new staff appointee, Gordon Ricketts, a year after it had been requested. Then while Sheppard and, subsequently, Ricketts immediately showed intelligent involvement, there was no improvement readily observable.

In 1958, at another crowded annual general meeting attended by numerous persons from the provinces, the RIBA council was once again censured from the floor. Condemning its business inefficiency, the resolution demanded that it be reformed to make it more representative of the general membership.* Ronald Bradbury, who three years earlier had assured the meeting that his colleagues were doing their best for everyone, once again voiced the views of the prevailing order.

> Look at the personnel whose work you are criticising. Take some of the names. Looking at the names of the Council you will see Mr. Basil Spence, Sir Leslie Martin, Mr. Gibberd, Mr. Forshaw, Mr. F. R. S. Yorke, Mr. Brett, Mr. Sheppard and so on, people who are architects of tremendous scope and quality, who are entrusted with the handling by their clients of jobs worth millions and millions of pounds. You are suggesting that those people who are on the Council have just acted like a bunch of nitwits. You are suggesting that these members of your profession, men of outstanding ability architecturally and in the field of business, and with regard to any standard you like to judge them, have just behaved like nitwits.[174]

The membership was not impressed. It had become apparent that even if elected members had any control of events, to be a modern architect was in itself an insufficient accomplishment with which to solve the problems that were estranging the mass of ordinary members.

Voting 500 to 10, the meeting demanded change. Two months later Barr, who had moved the motion of censure, was elected chairman of a

*The honorary treasurer was E. D. Jefferiss Mathews who having three times unsuccessfully stood for election each time placing well down the list, was then appointed a vice-president and subsequently honorary treasurer. In 1959 he again stood for election, was again defeated, and so temporarily left the RIBA council as under the new impending rules the appointment could only go to an elected member.

constitutional committee set up to review the whole organizational structure of the RIBA; soon afterwards, Ricketts was designated secretary to take over from the retiring Spragg. In the years following, the RIBA proceeded to assimilate the Allied Societies and redistribute its membership into branch, regional and national groupings through which all council members could be elected. The council itself elected the president who gathered from its members a cabinet-type policy committee advised by staff departments on a civil service pattern. Special interest groups such as official and salaried employees were encouraged to establish their own associations while principals were given practical guidance with the publication of the *Handbook of Architectural Practice and Management.** Educational standards were raised and schools of architecture steered into university faculties. Of major impetus, the survey into the organization, staffing, quality of service and productivity of *The Architect and his Office*, published in 1962, noting that only one in nine of the offices visited achieved an overall excellence of performance and over a third of them were inefficient in their managerial functions, concluded that the RIBA should exercise greater control over architectural standards in return for the protection given by its scale of fees.

But as the decade proceeded, the RIBA leadership seemed to advance with growing complacency in its own progressive institutionalism, overlooking the wide new demands for participation in its policies by an increasingly educated and questioning society.

> Beneath the buildings of quality [complained Ian Nairn in *The Observer* in 1966] there is a soggy, shoddy mass of half-digested clichés, half-peeling facades, half-comfortable, untested preconceptions about what people want . . . It is as though, denied any real part in the building operation, the architect must assert himself somehow, at the viewers' expense . . .[175]

While the establishment could easily ignore the lay critic's attack, its controversial innovations were slowed down by unexpected internal dissent at the same time as the Labour government itself, jettisoning Socialist theory to economic stringency, threatened to induce competitiveness into the monopolistic practices of professional associations.

Although *The Architect and his Office* had shown that the profession

---

*The desire for an improved professional methodology is evidenced by the success of the elemental design guides published by *The Architects' Journal* from October 1961 on which reportedly caused a one-third increase in the magazine's readership.

was seriously deficient in coordinating skills (ingeniously adding that there was "no reason why architects should not turn out to be rather good at this sort of thing. Many of them, we believe, subconsciously are"),[176] the RIBA adhered to the belief that the architect was the natural leader of those teams that produced not only buildings but also communities and towns.

The impact of town and country planning had been diminished under the successive Conservative governments of the nineteen-fifties. Suppression of the ribbon development of buildings along highways and their consolidation into urban areas, coupled with the preservation of designated green belts and scenic localities, had produced an orderly countryside that was widely underrated because its virtues were mainly passive. Its inadequacies were more easily recognized.

One of the expressions of bewilderment that is most commonly heard in the profession [asserted the notable planner Thomas Sharp in 1957] . . . is that to most people planning has now become just a colossal bore and that to many others it is something actually to dislike with an active hostility. . . . what is most disliked about us . . . is the control which we exercise over other people's activities with so little obvious and acceptable result . . . It seems to me that our plans today are so small and dreary and are made known so dimly and grudgingly that in the main they deserve the indifference and even, perhaps, the contempt that they get . . . What the interested public . . . is becoming increasingly angry about, is that all over the country there is visual squalor and mess—mess which people believe it should be the planner's prime business to stop. But the mess doesn't stop. It seems to go on and on.[177]

The major failures were inside the urban areas. Graceless commercial buildings arose disjointedly along antiquated overcrowded streets; and while speculative housing spawned without social organization, council housing broke up communities into arbitrary estates. Without a solution to the problem of controlling the price of land, planning was largely the administration of controls by local government committees who, advised by their professional staffs, considered over a third of a million applications annually in an estimated average time of four minutes each. For architects encouraged in training to indulge in macroscopic conceptions, there was little appeal in this commonplace employment. Of 1200 architects in 1963 who were also chartered planners, 400 practised exclusively as planners and of these only 148 worked with local planning authorities.[178]

However, the profession argued, it was not that architects were unwilling to be planners but that planning as it was practised had turned its back on the comprehensive design that was naturally the extension of the architect's specialty. An interest in environmental planning was reactivated by the Society for the Promotion of Urban Renewal formed by various specialists in 1958 to focus attention on the need for suitably rebuilding cities; and although it disbanded five years later, the doctrines of its chairman, Lionel Brett, who as Lord Esher later became RIBA president, were officially adopted by the RIBA council in 1965 when, once again invoking the sophism that the architect's skill in the (aesthetically oriented) planned arrangement of buildings fitted him to plan (community oriented) urban areas which merely had somewhat more complex social, economic, engineering and other components, it recommended that substantial planning instruction be incorporated into architectural education.[179]

Simultaneously pressed by some of its leaders to accept the argument that planning was not a distinctive self-contained discipline but largely the application of other specialties to a complex activity, the ordinary membership of the Town Planning Institute used its votes to rebel, refusing its professional recognition of ostensibly related graduates and replacing their proponents on its council by those in favour of continued autonomy. But even though the Town Planning Institute could block the encroachment of the RIBA, it was nevertheless the architect-planners who got the paramount roles in the urbanization program.

While the advocates of new (and, less enthusiastically, extended) towns, the Reith Committee, had in their final report of 1946 suggested that the employment of town planners was undesirable and that planning should be carried out by a team of specialists presumably directed by the chief administrator, the government bill of that year made no provision for the appointment of officers, relying on the discretion of each development corporation.[180] The resultant use of architect-planners as the most convenient professionals available created substantial areas of designed environment.

Preceding the new towns (and the much later but then topical and influential Buchanan Report on *Traffic in Towns*), Coventry provided the first central area to free its citizens from the harassment of vehicles. Proposed by its architect Gibson soon after its destruction by bombing early in the war, the city's new centre extended over the years into a varied grouping of public functions and forms that include the cathedral designed by Basil Spence. The new town centres were slow in building due to the overriding need for housing, that of the first new town,

Stevenage, being constructed in the late nineteen-fifties. While similarly planned for traffic segregation, it lacks the mundane vitality of Coventry substituting a more disciplined layout and aesthetic reminiscent of earlier transatlantic shopping centres.

But even where centres were conceived as entities, there was still no architectural ordering of the urban conglomeration. The urge for a new image of the city to supplant the garden city ideal resulted in two town designs that changed the fashionable pattern of urban form. Designed almost concurrently and linked both informally and through the shared services of their landscape consultant, the new town of Cumbernauld (the first to be designated by the Conservative government, in 1956) and the London County Council projected new town of Hook (initiated in 1957) both set out to create an environment indicative of twentieth century living. Although the Hook study was abandoned in 1960 when implementation was refused by the cooperating county, its imagery, perhaps even more potent in sketches than if built, was propagated through its later publication.[181] By then the new form was rising on a hilltop in Scotland where Cumbernauld was being constructed under the direction of Hugh Wilson.

Roughly five miles long and two miles wide, Cumbernauld is scheduled to have an eventual population of seventy thousand to alleviate congestion in Glasgow fifteen miles to the west. The town was conceived as an urban cluster with a southern industrial edge, surrounded by peripheral recreational areas and set within a backdrop of open hilly country. Two miles long and one mile wide, the dense ridge development contains 45,000 persons, the remaining population being accommodated in satellite villages and other industry placed at its northern extremity. With all parts of the central area within reasonable walking distance, a footpath system passes over or under main roads where they cross and ensures complete insulation from fast moving traffic. Along these walkways are located general stores, churches, pubs, primary schools and other local community facilities including playgrounds for older children, while preschool playspaces are set within groups of housing planned with separate vehicular and pedestrian access. The road system, based on an assumed ownership of over one car per family, is organized on a hierarchy of usages with interchanges at important intersections, the interurban highways connecting to a dual carriageway that passes under and rings part of the central area and connects to a single carriageway circling the town's housing. The intention has been to balance the high densities of the residential areas by their closeness to open country beyond and the town centre within which, built over parking for 5000 cars, contains in its multilevel structure reached by escalators, elevators and ramps, the major shopping, business, entertainment and public facilities for the entire community.[182]

That Cumbernauld is a success is evidenced by the approval of over eighty-seven percent of its inhabitants and its receipt of the 1967 R. S. Reynolds Memorial Award as the best example of community architecture in the world. However, it may be argued that by obtaining the urban character that its architects desired, it has established standards of size, access and proximity that might easily become obsolete even before the expiration of its amortization period of sixty years if Britain's standard of living improves at a rate equal to that of other western countries. It seems unreasonable to assume that the desire for increased material comfort will stop at the purchase of a car without affecting other social habits: that the housewife will not soon object to turning her back on the prestigious interchanges of her (husband's) urban motorways while daily pushing her pram up ramps through mist and rain; that the new car-owning community for which Cumbernauld is specifically designed will not also expect something more than the huddling of minimal dwellings, the drab apartment building entrance halls (even to the so-called luxury penthouses), and even something more aesthetic than the incredibly crude structural and servicing components of the first phase of the town centre which contrast so significantly with the consumer-oriented linings of the rented volumes.*

Thus it might be contended that the physical effect of unity is socially specious being based on a concocted urban construct that has been built up from architecturally fashionable technical solutions to un-related problems that do not originate from similar elements of society. And that then having been tied to a workingclassness by the unique circumstances of its settlement, Cumbernauld has restrictively embodied this lowest common denominator into its long-term physical image.

Another five years passed before the Conservative government designated its second new town Skelmersdale to relieve congestion in the Liverpool area. Then national exigencies and local pressures reactivated an accelerating involvement in economic and physical planning that was naturally continued by the succeeding Labour government. Modern architects of major repute produced designs for whole regions that appear to augur a new period of achievement.† But

---

*The low environmental level of public volumes in the first phase of the new town centre should be contrasted with the high public standard set by new British Railway stations and trains.

†For example, the partnership of Wilson and Womersley which formed in

stimulating projects often make disagreeable reality and history ends with evidence not prophecy.

As I go around the country [R. H. S. Crossman, a former Minister of Housing and Local Government, once observed] . . . I am getting used to being shown the most magnificent plans in the council offices and then feeling a sense of anti-climax when I walk outside and see the actual buildings going up . . . Of course this is not surprising. The genius of a Wren is always rare; talent is never plentiful and even competence is uncommon enough. In the world of architecture and engineering we certainly do not have a tremendous amount of talent available, and it seems to me that the little we have we are not using sensibly . . . but just imagine what our country would look like if we had no Town and Country Planning . . . We have only to reflect on the American scene . . . [183]

1962 has prepared central area plans for Exeter, Oxford, Brighton and Cardiff; master plans for the new towns of Skelmersdale, Redditch, and Irvine and the expanded town of Northampton; and proposals for the Northampton-Bedford region and the Teesside.

REFERENCES

The main magazine sources are:

The Architect and Building News (A & BN)
The Architects' Journal (AJ)
Architectural Association Journal (AAJ)
Architectural Design (AD)
The Architectural Review (AR)
Royal Institute of British Architects Journal (RIBAJ)

Statistics, unless otherwise noted, are derived from governmental or institutional sources.

[1] Reginald Blomfield, "Is modern architecture on the right track?", a symposium, *The Listener*, X, 1933, p. 124. See also Reginald Blomfield and A. D. Connell, "For and against modern architecture", *The Listener*, XII, 1934, pp. 885–888.

[2] P. M. Stratton, "The line from France", AR, LXIV, 1928, p. 1.

[3] Howard Robertson, *The Principles of Architectural Composition*, London 1924, p. 117. See also Howard Robertson, *Architecture Explained*, London 1926.

[4] Howard Robertson, "Obbligato to architecture", *The Builder*, CCII, 1962, pp. 854–855.

[5] Howard Robertson and F. R. Yerbury, "The housing exhibition at Stuttgart", A & BN, CXVIII, 1927, p. 766.

[6] Le Corbusier, *Towards a New Architecture*, London 1927.

[7] Stratton, "The line from France", p. 1.

[8] "Modern architecture", *The Times Literary Supplement*, XXVI, 1927, p. 734.

[9] S.C.R., A & BN, CXVIII, 1927, p. 950.

[10] Harold Tomlison, "Towards a new architecture", AJ, LXVI, 1927, p. 378.

[11] *The Book of the Liverpool School of Architecture*, edited by Lionel B. Budden, Liverpool 1932; C. H. Reilly, *Architectural Problems*, Liverpool 1924.

[12] Gilbert H. Jenkins, "Modernism in architecture", AAJ, XLIII, 1927, p. 160.

[13] R. A. Duncan, "Modernism in architecture", discussion, *ibid.*, p. 169.

[14] Howard Robertson, "An experiment with time", A & BN, CXXIII, 1930, p. 12.

[15] Christopher Hussey, *Country Life*, LX, 1931, p. 307.

[16] A & BN, CXXXIII, 1933, p. 314.

[17] *Ibid.*, pp. 316–317.

[18] Museum of Modern Art, *Modern Architecture, International Exhibition*, New York 1932.

[19] A. L. Roberts, "The panel system. How it works", AJ, LXXIX, 1934, pp. 935–936; Giles Gilbert Scott and Percy Hurd, "The advisory panel system", AJ, LXXX, 1934, p. 258.

[20] "The first round", A & BN, CXXII, 1929, pp. 608–609.

[21] "The Ruislip case. The full history", AJ, LXXIX, 1934, pp. 786–787.

[22] "The Ruislip case", AJ, LXXIX, 1934, p. 747.

[23] "The Ruislip result", AJ, LXXIX, 1934, p. 743.

[24] E. Maxwell Fry, "English architecture from the 'thirties", Architects Year Book 8, 1957, p. 54.

[25] "Connell, Ward and Lucas, 1927–1939", AAJ, LXXII, 1956, pp. 94–115.

[26] P. Morton Shand, "Wine cellar design in the private house", AJ, LXIV, 1926, pp. 26–27.

[27] P. Morton Shand, "Stockholm, 1930", AR, LXVIII, 1930, p. 68. See also "Writings on architecture by P. Morton Shand", AAJ, LXXV, 1959, pp. 134–192.

[28] Shand, "Stockholm, 1930", pp. 70–71.

[29] P. Morton Shand, "Salute to adventurers", AR, LXV, 1929, p. 17.

[30] Shand, "Stockholm, 1930", p. 72.

[31] "Lord Benbow's Apartments. Assessor's report", AR, LXVIII, 1930, p. 201.

[32] Ibid., pp. 202–203.

[33] Michael Dugdale, "The problem of modern architecture", AR, LXXII, 1932, p. 101.

[34] R. A. Duncan, "Modern architectural design", AJ, LXXVI, 1932, p. 165. See also R. A. Duncan, The Architecture of a New Era, London 1933. Another interesting book of this period is Clough William-Ellis and John Summerson, Architecture Here and Now, London 1934.

[35] F. R. S. Yorke, "New work on London's underground stations", AJ, LXXVI, 1932, pp. 819–826.

[36] Extract from a letter written by Sigfried Giedion to Wells Coates, AJ, LXXX, 1934, p. 425. In the publications of the Congrès Internationaux d'Architecture Moderne, Wohnung Für Das Existenzminimum, Frankfurt 1930, and Rationelle Bebauungsweissen, Stuttgart 1931, the English delegate was listed as C. J. Robertson and H. Robertson respectively.

[37] "MARS at Olympia", AJ, LXXX, 1934, p. 425.

[38] Geoffrey Ridley, "Architecture and town planning", Twelve Studies in Soviet Russia, edited by Margaret I. Cole, London 1933; Art in the U.S.S.R., edited by C. G. Holme, London 1935; Osip Beskin, The Place of Art in the Soviet Union, New York 1936.

[39] "The Russian Scene", AR, LXXI, 1932, pp. 173–214.

[40] Le Corbusier's comments on "the chosen few" are taken from Towards a New Architecture, p. 96, and on his Palace of the Soviets project from Le Corbusier et Pierre Jeanneret, Oeuvre Complète de 1929–1934, Zurich 1935, p. 13.

[41] Stephen H. Roberts, The House that Hitler Built, London 1937. See also Adolf Hitler, "Art and politics", Liberty Art Nationhood, Berlin 1935, pp. 33–53; Vaso Trivanovitch, Economic Development of Germany under National Socialism, New York 1937.

[42] Oswald Mosley, The Greater Britain, [London 1932]; Colin Cross, The Fascists in Britain, London 1961.

[43] Herbert W. Robinson, The Economics of Building, London 1939, appendix 2.

[44] "President's appeal for relief fund", RIBAJ, XXXIX, 1931, p. 138.

[45] AJ, LXXIX, 1934, p. 244.

[46] "The admission of foreign architects to practise in England", RIBAJ, XLI,

1934, p. 384. See also "Refugees Committee. Report to Council", RIBAJ, XLVI, 1939, pp. 826–831.

[47] "Question to Sir Oswald Mosley", AJ, LXXIX, 1934, p. 269.

[48] "Replies to 'Question to Sir Oswald Mosley' ", AJ, LXXIX, 1934, pp. 566–567.

[49] Berthold Lubetkin, "Architectural thought since the revolution", AR, LXXI, 1932, p. 201. See also R. Furneaux Jordan, "Lubetkin", CXVIII, 1955, pp. 36–44.

[50] Le Corbusier, "The vertical garden city", AR, LXXIX, 1936, p. 10.

[51] Anthony Cox, "Highpoint Two, North Hill, Highgate", Focus, II, 1938, p. 79.

[52] Lubetkin, "Architectural thought since the revolution", p. 207.

[53] "Highpoint Number Two", AR, LXXXIV, 1938, p. 166.

[54] J. M. Richards, "Towards a rational aesthetic", AR, LXXVIII, 1935, pp. 211–218.

[55] J. M. Richards, "The condition of architecture and the principle of anonymity", Circle, edited by J. L. Martin et al., London 1937, p. 184.

[56] Richards, "Towards a rational aesthetic", p. 216.

[57] J. M. Richards, "Modern architecture and the public" AR, LXXXI, 1937, p. 203.

[58] Harold Tomlison, "Towards a new architecture", p. 379.

[59] J. M. Richards, An Introduction to Modern Architecture, Penguin Books, London 1940, p. 15.

[60] Richards, "Towards a rational aesthetic", p. 212.

[61] Ibid., p. 213.

[62] F. R. S. Yorke and Colin Penn, A Key to Modern Architecture, London 1939, p. 45.

[63] F. R. S. Yorke, The Modern House, London 1934, p. 14.

[64] "Felix James Samuely", AAJ, LXXVI, 1960, pp. 2–31. See also R. B. White, Qualitative Studies of Buildings, National Building Studies special report 39, London 1966.

[65] "News Chronicle Schools Competition", AJ, LXXXV, 1937, pp. 511–544.

[66] Hitchcock, "Modern architecture in England", p. 25.

[67] Leeds School of Architecture, AJ, LXXXVI, 1937, pp. 60–61, 980; Liverpool School of Architecture, AJ, LXXXVI, 1937, pp. 91, 110.

[68] J. E., "Mr. H. S. Goodhart-Rendel. An appreciation", AAJ, LIV, 1938, p. 100. See also John Summerson, The Architectural Association 1847–1947, London 1947, pp. 46–49; The Editors, "The AA story", Focus, III, 1939, pp. 79–111.

[69] MARS group, New Architecture, London 1938, p. 6.

[70] "Exhibition by the Mars group", The Times, 13 January 1938, p. 10.

[71] Le Corbusier, Urbanisme, Paris 1924.

[72] A. Trystan Edwards, "The dead city", AR, LXVI, 1929, p. 137.

[73] "The problem of the great city", The Studio, XCVIII, 1929, p. 611.

[74] Parliamentary Debates, House of Commons, CCLXI, 1932, cc. 41–42.

[75] William Ashworth, The Genesis of Modern British Town Planning, London 1954.

[76] Royal Institute of British Architects, International Architecture 1924–1934, London 1934, p. 9.

[77] Ministry of Works and Planning, Committee on Land Utilisation in Rural Areas, Report, London 1942, pp. 20 and 53. See also C. E. M. Joad, About Education, London 1945, pp. 130–137.

O

[78] Wells Coates, *Unit One: The Modern Movement in English Architecture, Painting and Sculpture*, edited by Herbert Read, London 1934, p. 108. See also J. M. Richards, "Wells Coates 1893–1958", AR, CXXIV, 1958, pp. 357–360.

[79] Raymond McGrath, *International Architecture 1924–1934*, p. 56.

[80] "MARS at Olympia", AJ, LXXX, 1934, pp. 425–426.

[81] McGrath, *International Architecture 1924–1934*, pp. 59–60.

[82] Yorke, *The Modern House*, p. 5.

[83] Raymond McGrath, *Twentieth Century Houses*, p. 210.

[84] E. Maxwell Fry, "The small house of today", AR, LXXVI, 1934, p. 20.

[85] John Strachey, *The Menace of Fascism*, London 1933.

[86] Letter to the Editor from students from the Slade School, Chelsea Art School, Willesden Art School, Bartlett School of Architecture, Royal College of Art and the Architectural Association School of Architecture, AJ, LXXXIV, 1936, p. 740.

[87] Serge Chermayeff and J. M. Richards, "A hundred years ahead", AJ, LXXXI, 1935, p. 81.

[88] Letter to the Editor from Keith Aitken, AJ, LXXXI, 1935, pp. 159–160.

[89] Editorial note, AJ, LXXXI, 1935, p. 264.

[90] Letter to the Editor from Serge Chermayeff and J. M. Richards, AJ, LXXXI, 1935, pp. 189–190.

[91] Letter to the Editor from F. Skinner, AJ, LXXXI, 1935, p. 188.

[92] Chermayeff and Richards, "A hundred years ahead", p. 81.

[93] Serge Chermayeff, "The future for students", AJ, LXXXI, 1935, p. 435.

[94] "The Hertford Competition; diverse outlooks", AJ, LXXXII, 1935, p. 627.

[95] Astragal, AJ, LXXXII, 1935, p. 616.

[96] Berthold Lubetkin, "Modern architecture in England", *American Architect and Architecture*, CL, 1937, p. 30.

[97] "Working class housing exhibition at the Housing Centre", AJ, LXXXIII, 1936, p. 609.

[98] "The A.T.O. Bulletin", AJ, LXXXIII, 1936, p. 958.

[99] Architects and Technicians Organisation, *Summary of Work 1934–6*, 1936.

[100] Harold Bellman, "The building trades", *Britain in Recovery*, London 1938, pp. 395–437; Marian Bowley, *Housing and the State 1919–1944*, London 1945; Ministry of Health, *Private Enterprise Housing*, London 1944.

[101] National Housing Committee, *Housing and Planning Policy. Interim Report*, London 1936, pp. 5–9. See also National Housing Committee, *A National Housing Policy*, London 1934; B. S. Townroe, *Britain Rebuilding*, London 1936.

[102] *Royal Commission on the Distribution of the Industrial Population. Report*, Cmd. 6153, London 1940, p. 3.

[103] *Ibid.*, p. 194.

[104] *Ibid.*, p. 189.

[105] *Ibid.*, pp. 219–221.

[106] *Ibid.*, pp. 225–226.

[107] Unit 15 of the AA School, "The MARS exhibition", AAJ, LIII, 1938, pp. 387–388.

[108] "The A.A. S.T.A. report", AJ, LXXXVIII, 1938, p. 3. See also Association of Architects, Surveyors and Technical Assistants, *History of Architects*, London 1935; their various reports from 1938 onwards; and their magazine *Keystone*.

[109] Tecton, *Planned A.R.P.*, London 1939.

[110] *Focus*, I, 1938, p. 1.

[111] E. Stanley Hall, "The architect's task", RIBAJ, XLVII, 1939, p. 27.

[112] "Resolution", AJ, LXXXIX, 1939, p. 3.

[113] Letter to the Editor from Ian MacAlister, RIBAJ, XLVIII, 1941, p. 38.

[114] C. M. Kohan, *Works and Buildings*, London 1952; Ian Bowen, "The control of building", *Lessons of the British War Economy*, edited by D. N. Chester, Cambridge 1951, pp. 122–143; J. C. W. Reith, *Into the Wind*, London 1949, pp. 405–445.

[115] John Dower, "The Barlow report", RIBAJ, XLVII, 1940, p. 101.

[116] J. C. W. Reith, *Parliamentary Debates, House of Lords*, CXVIII, 1941, c. 514.

[117] Reconstruction Committee, "First general statement of conclusions", RIBAJ, XLIX, 1942, p. 165.

[118] "Arthur Korn 1891 to the present day", AAJ, LXXIII, 1957, pp. 114–118.

[119] Lionel Brett, "Doubts on the MARS plan for London", AJ, XCVI, 1942, pp. 24–25.

[120] Letter to the Editor from M. Hartland Thomas, AJ, C, 1944, p. 39. See also MARS group, *Observations on the County of London Plan*, Report No. 2, 1944.

[121] Letter to the Editor of *The Times* from Percy Thomas quoted in "The County of London plan", RIBAJ, L, 1943, p. 193.

[122] J. H. Forshaw and Patrick Abercrombie, *County of London Plan*, London 1943.

[123] Winston Churchill, *The Times*, 27 March 1944, p. 8.

[124] Astragal, AJ, C, 1944, p. 394.

[125] "Housing and town planning after the war", *The Builder*, CI, 1943, p. 376; *Your Home. Planned by Labour*, 1943; Ellen Wilkinson, *Plan for Peace*, [1945]; Ernest Bevin, *Parliamentary Debates, House of Commons*, CDX, 1945, p. 958; Ministry of Reconstruction, *Housing*, Cmd. 6609, London 1945; Winston Churchill, *Here is the Course We Steer*, 1945.

[126] Aneurin Bevan, *Parliamentary Debates, House of Commons*, CDXIV, 1945, cc. 1218–1234; Paul F. Wendt, *Housing Policy—the Search for Solutions*, Berkeley 1962.

[127] Ministry of Education, *The Story of Post-War School Building*, London 1957.

[128] "Housing Manual, 1949", AJ, CX, 1949, p. 577. See also Ministry of Health, *Housing Manual*, London 1944.

[129] "The grand patron of the architect", AJ, CXIV, 1951, p. 489.

[130] "Housing and town planning after the war", p. 376.

[131] MARS group, *What is Modern Architecture*, Report No. 3, 1945.

[132] "The new Crystal Palace", AR, XCIX, 1946, p. lxiii.

[133] Le Corbusier, "Crystal Palace", *Architects Year Book* 2, 1947, p. 148.

[134] Duncan Sandys, "Address by the Minister of Works", RIBAJ, LII, 1945, p. 215.

[135] Aneurin Bevan, AJ, CII, 1945, p. 253; Ministry of Works, *House Construction, Third Report*, Post-war building study No. 25; Ministry of Works, *New Methods of House Construction*, Special report No. 4, London 1948.

[136] A. W. Cleeve Barr, *Public Authority Housing*, B. T. Batsford Ltd, London 1958.

[137] Ministry of Works, *Temporary Housing Programme*, Cmd. 6686, London 1945; Ministry of Works, *Temporary Housing Programme*, Cmd. 7304, London 1948.

[138] Ministry of Works, *Standard Construction for Schools*, Post-war building study No. 2, London 1944, p. 1. See also C. G. Stillman, "Schools", AJ, XCVI, 1942, pp. 342–351; Eric L. Bird, "The post-war schools of the Hertfordshire County Council", RIBAJ, LVI, 1949, pp. 471–479; Guy Oddie, "The new

English humanism", AR, CXXXIV, 1963, pp. 180–182; and Letter to the Editor from Guy Oddie, AR, CXXXVI, 1964, p. 397.

139 Ministry of Education, *New Primary Schools*, Building bulletin No. 1, London 1949, p. 44.

140 Royal Institute of British Architects, *Committee to Consider the Present and Future of Private Architectural Practice*, London 1950, p. 12.

141 Lloyd Rodwin, *The British New Towns Policy*, Cambridge 1956.

142 J. M. Richards, "Failure of the new towns", AR, CXIV, 1953, p. 32; Lionel Brett, "Failure of the new towns. A reply", AR, CXIV, 1953, pp. 119–120.

143 J. M. Richards, *The Castles on the Ground*, London 1946, p. 15.

144 H. S. Goodhart-Rendel, "Inaugural address", RIBAJ, XLV, 1937, p. 9. See also H. S. Goodhart-Rendel, "Rebuilding after the war", A & BN, CLXXII, 1942, pp. 123–126, 136–138.

145 "Analysis of architects' employment", RIBAJ, XLVII, 1940, p. 50; *Report of the Committee to Consider the Present and Future of Private Architectural Practice*, p. 31.

146 Gerald Barry, "The Festival of Britain 1951", *Royal Society of Arts Journal*, C, 1952, p. 688. See also "South Bank exhibition", AR, CX, 1951, pp. 72–138.

147 "Modern architecture makes good", AJ, CXIII, 1951, p. 619.

148 A. E. Richardson, "Festival architecture", *Building*, XXVI, 1951, p. 209.

149 Ian Bowen, "Focus on you. Results of the sample survey", AJ, CXVIII, 1953, pp. 468–470.

150 Letter to the Editor from Hugh Pope, AR, CXV, 1954, p. 364.

151 "Team 10 primer", AD, XXXII, 1962, p. 566.

152 Letter to the Editor from Richard Llewelyn Davies and John Weeks, AR, CXVI, 1954, p. 2.

153 John Summerson, introduction to Trevor Dannatt, *Modern Architecture in Britain*, B. T. Batsford Ltd, London 1959, p. 28.

154 "The New Brutalism", AJ, CXX, 1954, p. 336. See also K. J. Bolton, "Hunstanton Secondary Modern School", *Era*, 1 (No. 3), 1968, pp. 34–37.

155 Peter Smithson, "Futurism and modern architecture", discussion, RIBAJ, LXIV, 1957, p. 137.

156 Denys Lasdun, "Mars group 1953–1957", *Architects' Year Book 8*, 1957, pp. 57–60.

157 Reyner Banham, "Apropos the Smithsons", *New Statesman*, LXII, 1961, pp. 317–318. See also Reyner Banham, *The New Brutalism. Ethic or Aesthetic?*, London 1966; Royston Landau, *New Directions in British Architecture* New York, 1968.

158 "Le Corbusier's Unité d'Habitation", AR, CIX, 1951, pp. 293–300. See also R. Furneaux Jordan, "L.C.C. New standards in official architecture", AR, CXX, 1956, pp. 302–324.

159 Letter to the Editor from F. Samuely, AJ, CXXIII, 1955, pp. 222–223. See also Eric S. Benson, "Precast concrete in framed structures", RIBAJ, LXIII, 1956, pp. 145–149.

160 Ministry of Housing and Local Government, *Homes for Today and Tomorrow*, London 1961, pp. 1–2, 5–6.

161 *Ibid.*, p. 37.

162 AR, CXVII, 1955, p. 6.

163 Robin Boyd, "The engineering of excitement", AR, CXXIV, 1958, pp. 294–306.

164 "No future in the town hall", AR, CXXXVIII, 1965, p. 245.

165 "Architects' architecture", AJ, CXXXIX, 1964, pp. 126–165.

REFERENCES

[166] John Jacobus, "Engineering Building, Leicester University", AR, CXXXV, 1964, p. 254.

[167] "Hertfordshire's hundredth new school", RIBAJ, LXII, 1955, p. 134.

[168] Elizabeth Layton, *Building by Local Authorities*, London 1961.

[169] Ministry of Education, *The Story of Clasp*, Building bulletin No. 19, London 1961.

[170] Peter Trench, "Looking ahead at the building industry", RIBAJ, LXVII, 1960, p. 367. See also "Pre-IBSAC symposium", AJ, CXXXIX, 1964, pp. 1413–1436; RIBA, *The Industrialization of Building*, London 1965. R. B. White, *Prefabrication: A history of its development in Great Britain*, National Building Studies special report 36, London 1965.

[171] Ministry of Works, *Survey of Problems before the Construction Industries*, London 1962, See also O. W. Roskill, *The Building Industry . . . 1962 Onward*, a survey by *The Builder*, London 1962.

[172] "NBA. Ten ways of helping", AJ, CXLV, 1967, pp. 1390–1391.

[173] "Report of the committee on the constitution of the council", RIBAJ, LIX, 1952, pp. 279–281. See also "Final report of the constitutional committee", RIBAJ, LXVII, 1960, pp. 319–325.

[174] R. Bradbury, "Annual General Meeting", discussion, RIBAJ, LXV, 1958, p. 266.

[175] Ian Nairn, "Stop the architects now", *The Observer*, 13 February 1966, p. 21.

[176] RIBA, *The Architect and his Office*, London 1962, p. 181.

[177] Thomas Sharp, "Planning now", *Town Planning Institute, Journal*, XLIII, 1957, pp. 133–136. See also "Failure of planning", *The Sunday Times*, 9 August 1964, p. 10.

[178] J. B. Cullingworth, *Town and Country Planning in England and Wales*, London 1964; "The architect in town planning", RIBAJ, LXX, 1963, pp. 243–246.

[179] Lionel Brett, "The environmentalists", AR, CXXV, 1959, pp. 303–305. "Lord Esher, the RIBA president 1965–66, talks to the editor of the RIBA Journal", RIBAJ, LXXII, 1965, p. 337; "An RIBA policy for planning", RIBAJ, LXXII, 1965, pp. 223–230. See also Lewis B. Keeble, "Presidential address 1965", *Town Planning Institute, Journal*, LI, 1965, pp. 356–362.

[180] Ministry of Town and Country Planning, *Final Report of the New Towns Committee*, Cmd. 6876, London 1946.

[181] London County Council, *The Planning of a New Town*, London 1961.

[182] Cumbernauld Development Corporation, *Cumbernauld Technical Brochure*; University of Strathclyde, Cumbernauld 67: *A Household Survey and Report*.

[183] R. H. S. Crossman, "Planning policies of the government", *Town Planning Institute, Journal*, LI, 1965, pp. 206–207.

INDEX